SELECTED POEMS OF
JOSEPH SKIPSEY
(1832-1903)

Frontispiece to Miscellaneous Lyrics, *Bedlington, printed for the author by George Richardson (1878)*

SELECTED POEMS OF JOSEPH SKIPSEY (1832-1903)

Selected by
WILLIAM DANIEL MCCUMISKEY and R. K. R. THORNTON
with introductory biographical notes on Skipsey
revised and augmented by
CHRIS HARRISON and R. K. R. THORNTON

RECTORY PRESS
2014

To be had from R. K. R. Thornton at the
Rectory Press,
2 Rectory Terrace,
Gosforth,
Newcastle upon Tyne NE3 1XY
England

rkrthornton@btinternet.com

Edition limited to 100 copies.

ISBN 978-0-9572415-2-7

Typeset in Palatino and printed in England on recycled paper by
Imprintdigital

In memory of Alice Edwards McCumiskey
(née Clapperton, 1920-2011),
who said
'There is often a fine heart under a raggy shirt'.

PERCY PIT, PERCY MAIN COLLIERY.

Drawn by T.H. Hair. Etched by J. Smith.

CONTENTS

Skipsey's life and experience were unquestionably dramatic – his father's murder when he was a babe in arms, his self-education down the pit from the age of seven, the glittering array of supporters for his candidacy for the curatorship of Shakespeare's birthplace and his relinquishing it after only two years. But rather than make a sensational account, we have presented the plain facts as far as we can find them and let them speak for themselves. Thus we have often followed the story simply by quotation of the documents from which our facts are drawn. The material may seem a little repetitive; but there are important nuances to each account, and much of the material is hard to come by, so we have preferred to quote fully rather than summarize.

Robert Spence Watson's biography of Skipsey gives most of the basic facts. The gerald-massey.org.uk website with its input from Skipsey's descendants is immensely helpful (correcting some of Basil Bunting's slips and adding valuable detail), and Roger Skipsey, the poet's great grandson, has provided welcome help in getting pictures and generously allowing us to use them. Newcastle City Library's access to the Nineteenth-Century periodical database has allowed searches of the periodical literature, which has filled out many details in the story; while the e-journal facility of Newcastle University's Robinson Library has allowed us to check some of Skipsey's appearances in periodicals. The fascinating website of the Durham Mining Museum has given us a good deal on the mining background. Skipsey's scrapbooks in the City Library of Newcastle upon Tyne are full of material unavailable anywhere else; and the Robinson Library Special Collections include Skipsey material in the Spence Watson collection. We are grateful to all the staff of these libraries who have been extremely helpful, and have given us permission to use material which is in their care. Thanks also to Hilary Thornton and Alistair Elliot, who gave welcome and refreshing overviews of the whole and saved us from a number of inaccuracies.

If the introductory notes do not fully convey how impressive a man Skipsey was, an impression that grows the more you read about him, it is worth noting that he was vividly remembered by everyone he met – Rossetti, Burne-Jones, William Morris, and the rest – and the testimony of such a notable figure as Robert Spence Watson cannot be ignored. Spence Watson wrote in his biography that Skipsey 'was indeed a rare conversationalist. No one who really knew him at all intimately could fail to see how much greater a man he was than even the best of his works showed him to be' (p.101). The impression is echoed by Ernest Rhys, who, as the editor of the 'Everyman' editions for J. M. Dent, must have known many writers, and says in his *Everyman Remembers* that, alongside William Morris, Walt Whitman, Rabindranath Tagore and George McDonald, Joseph Skipsey was 'one of the four or five most impressive, most convincingly self-impersonating figures among all the poets I have known' (p.90). Spence Watson sums up Skipsey by saying that: 'Looking back at him now that four years have passed since he left us, and taking him all in all, I think I have never known a greater man' (p.111).

Gosforth 2012

SECOND EDITION 2014

Chris Harrison, a great great grandson of the poet, has collaborated in this revision, adding information on Cuthbert Skipsey, on Joseph Skipsey's background, on his friendship with Thomas Dixon, and on his time at Stratford. We have taken the opportunity also to add material about his first book, and to correct a mistaken identification, where we said that a photograph of Spence Watson and his wife was Skipsey and his wife.

We would like to thank Simon Marshall of the Stone Gallery, 93 The High Street, Burford, Oxfordshire OX18 4QA, for his kind permission to use material from the Dixon-Skipsey correspondence. The *Shakespeare Birthplace Trust Collections* have also graciously given permission to use material in their possession: references after quotations to *SBT Collections* give the locations in that archive.

2014

JOSEPH SKIPSEY 1832-1903
BIOGRAPHICAL NOTES

Thus by his slow smouldering muse, his balladry and his uncouth northern speech he got hold of other poets' imaginations and became a legend.
Ernest Rhys, *Everyman Remembers*: pp.228-9

The recent welcome and deserved international fame of *The Pitmen Painters*, Lee Hall's play about the Ashington Group of painters, is in danger of perpetuating that common antithesis between the intellectual and the working man, between the man of culture and the man of work, as if it is a cause for surprise when a pitman paints a picture or writes a poem. Such an attitude affects many of our labourer poets – John Clare was marketed as the 'Northamptonshire Peasant Poet' for example. Our experience suggests (and we imagine Lee Hall's does as well) that the opposition of worker and artist is a false one, and we have found that the mining communities of Northumberland and Durham had (and have) a ferocious appetite for knowledge and culture. There are sophisticated workers as often as there are uncultured aristocrats, and the writer of the poems from which we present a selection is a good example of the former, a man who could hold his own among the guests at the dinner table of Robert Spence Watson just as well as he could hew a seam.

Joseph Skipsey was born on 17 March 1832 at Percy Main Colliery, the eighth child of Cuthbert and Isabella Skipsey. His father had a good job as an overman, but, as Richard Fynes tells us in his *Miners of Northumberland and Durham* (1873, p. 33), he was killed during a bitter strike.

> At a meeting of men on strike which took place at Chirton, near North Shields, on the 8th of July [1832], an affray took place between them and the special constables. Mr. Cuthbert Skipsey, a miner belonging to Percy Main, who bore the character of being a very

quiet, inoffensive man, at this time was trying to make peace between the parties, when George Weddle, a policeman, drew his pistol and deliberately shot him dead on the spot. Mr. Skipsey was a man very much respected at the colliery where he lived, and by his tragic end a widow and six children were left to the protection of the public.

Responses to the murder of Cuthbert Skipsey differ significantly, largely depending on which side of this highly charged situation the teller or the hearer stands. The pitmen were defending their jobs against others brought in when they refused to sign up to the coal-owners' conditions.

The *Newcastle Journal* for the 14th July 1832 described the setting at the inquest in some detail, and, although the paper was not generally a supporter of the miners' cause, gave them some credit for their behaviour during the inquest:

> We have witnessed many inquests, but never any that presented so peculiar an appearance as the one under notice at the moment of the Coroner opening the proceedings. The jury were arranged together on one side the room [*sic*], to the Coroner's right. Parrallel [*sic*] with them sat several of the weeping friends of the deceased. Opposite the Coroner was Mr. Lowry, of South Shields, the pitmen's professional adviser. Near him, on a form, directly facing the jury, were Benj. Pyle, Ralph Atkinson, and other delegates and demagogues of the Pitmen's Union. There was a crowd of pitmen outside; and many were entertaining themselves in the rooms below, while the avenues to the inquest room and the space within, near the door, were crowded to excess, all of whom we understood to be pitmen. Among these persons Hepburn,[1] (whose influence, as head of the Union has made him notorious) might be occasionally seen, and soon after the commencement of the proceedings, he joined his brother delegates, and remained facing the jury the remainder of the day. We may here remark, that with the exception of an occasional under-growl while the policemen were under examination, the conduct of the pitmen

---

[1] Thomas Hephurn (c1795-1864) formed the miners' union (the Northern Union of Pitmen, covering Northumberland and Durham) in 1830 and led the miners in the campaigns of 1831 and 1832.

was exemplary. As connected with the coal-trade we observed but one gentleman present, viz. George Johnson, Esq. colliery viewer for Burdon Main.

The Northumberland Advertiser, abridged in the *Examiner* for 15 July 1832, reported that on the 7th [it was in fact the 8th] a drunken pitman had shouted at some passing special constables who had been stationed at Burdon Main Colliery. When he said that they were blacklegs, they went back and collared him, upon which a boy went into a pub and informed the pitmen there drinking that their comrade had been arrested. They immediately came out to rescue their fellow workman, who ran off. The special constables fired after him to no effect. Then, the piece continues, they

> severely beat two of the pitmen near them with the but ends of their guns. After this had occurred a collier named Cuthbert Skipsey came up, and laying his hand on the shoulder of one of the policemen said "My man, you'd better go away and let's keep quiet." The policeman pushed him away, using a brutal expression, and immediately shot at him. The man staggered and fell and immediately expired. Some of the other men were taken into custody. The deceased was a peaceable, sober man, and has left a wife and eight children. The *Northumberland Advertiser* from which we have abridged the foregoing account, comments with just severity upon the reckless and intemperate conduct of the police on the occasion.

The *Caledonian Mercury* of 14 July 1832, quoting a report from the *Tyne Mercury*, tells a different story:

> On Sunday evening in consequence of some of the pitmen having threatened to prevent any of the men lately hired for Burdon Main colliery, near North Shields, from going to work there, Ralph Falcus and other constables went to afford protection to them and to the colliery. On their passing Dobson's public-house, a short distance from the village of Chirton, a pitman, who was sitting on the railway, used very abusive language towards them, and said, "Never a black-legged b----r should go to work that night." Falcus desired him to go away, but he would not, and finding remonstrance had no effect, he took him into custody. Immediately on this a number of pitmen

13

coming from the direction of Dobson's house, attacked the police officers, and forcibly rescued the prisoner from them. One of the constables, Matthew Raine, was knocked down, and a general scuffle took place. The pitmen had greatly the advantage in number, there being about thirty of them, while there were five only of the police. One of the pitmen of the name of Cuthbert Skipsey, endeavoured to wrest a pistol from George Weddell, a constable, and succeeded in throwing him on the ground. On this Matthew Raine struck Skipsey's hand and obliged him to release his hold. Weddell, thus relieved, retreated for some distance, but finding he was pursued by Skipsey he fired, and Skipsey staggered a few yards and fell down dead. These are the circumstances as far as we have been able to ascertain them.

At the trial for murder of George Weddell in Newcastle on 3rd August, both types of story were offered by prosecution and defence, and a rowdy group of pitmen in the court room hissed and yelled 'in a very indecorous manner' at some of the policemen's replies (report in the *Times*, issue 14923, 6 August 1832, p. 6, col D). The jury recorded a verdict of guilty but with a strong recommendation for mercy. Weddell was sentenced to six months hard labour. In his biography of Skipsey, Robert Spence Watson summed up in an even-handed manner when he wrote that 'Although the sentence seems to be a somewhat slight one, considering the excitement of the time and the whole facts of the case, and the not unnatural alarm of a special constable who found himself in an awkward and threatening position, the result was on the whole a satisfactory one. No one supposes there was any malice in the matter, which was the rash act of a man under great excitement and with the idea that he himself would probably be attacked' (p. 10).

Fynes, on the other hand, continues the account quoted above on pp.11-12, eager to make a contrast between the treatment of the miners and their oppressors, and so juxtaposes the case of Cuthbert Skipsey's killer with that of a miner who had killed a magistrate:

On August the 3rd, after a trial which continued about twelve hours, Weddle was found guilty of manslaughter and sentenced to six months imprisonment with hard labour. On the first of August, William Jobling was tried at the Durham assizes and found guilty of the murder of Nicholas Fairless as previously stated. He was sentenced to be hanged on the third, and his body to be afterwards hung in chains near the scene of the murder.

Whatever the rights and wrongs of the case, Isabella, Cuthbert's widow, was left with the hard job of bringing up a family of eight without a husband's wage – there is a story of Joseph being sent off to gather nettles for the cooking pot – and so the children were expected to bring in what they could earn at an early age. In 1839, the seven-year-old Joseph began work in the colliery as a 'trapper', opening the ventilation flaps ('traps') in the pit when the wagons went through and closing them afterwards to control the ventilation. This meant perhaps as long as sixteen hours a day, usually in darkness except when the wagons passed or a pitman gave him a candle end, but Skipsey, who had up to then only been taught the alphabet and how to put two letters together, used the time to teach himself to read and write by studying discarded playbills and advertisements and practising his writing on the traps themselves with a piece of chalk or with his finger in the dust. From these simple beginnings he graduated to the Bible, and then when he was fifteen to *Paradise Lost*, a copy of which an uncle lent him. From those he moved to the classic English poets and then to write his own poetry, publishing in local newspapers. The ballads that he learned from older lads in the pits stimulated his imagination. When he was seventeen, he acquired a copy of Shakespeare's works, which he saved for ten weeks to buy. Another relative, an aunt, helped him to understand the Shakespeare and she also lent him a copy of Burns, which had a powerful influence.

The Census taken in June 1841 was the first in the UK to name individuals and is helpful in telling us that Isabella Skipsey, widow (40), was living in Percy Main with her daughter Hannah (20), and sons Ja[me]s (11) and Joseph (9), both boys being listed as coal miners. By the 1851 Census Isabella, widow (51), was living at 51 Percy Main solely with Joseph, her son (19) who is recorded as a coal miner. They are both said to have been born in Wallsend.

In 1852, at the age of twenty, Skipsey went to London, walking a good part of the way, to get a labouring job. There was an enormous expanse in building of railways and railway stations in the metropolis, and Skipsey got a job connected with this work. While there he met his future wife, Sarah Ann Fendley, said to have been his landlady. She was one of a family of ten, and was born in October 1828 in Watlington, Norfolk, the daughter of Benjamin Fendley, agricultural labourer of the same village, and she had left home by the time she was 20. She was to bear Joseph eight children, but according to the marriage certificate they did not marry until 1868. Joseph and Sarah moved up to Coatbridge in Scotland, where he worked in the mines for six months, and then moved to Pemberton Collieries, near Sunderland. Spence Watson thought that Skipsey taught for a short time in one of the colliery villages (p. 23), but the money from fees was not sufficient, and he went back to the pit. Spence Watson records that he found work in Choppington, but offers no date. The Skipseys were back in Chirton by the time of the birth of their first son Cuthbert Skipsey, born on 12 January 1855. A second son, William, was born on 3 June 1857.

Joseph was already writing poems, many finding inspiration in the uncompleted snatches of songs of his fellow pitmen, which he felt a wish to complete; and he began to publish in the late 1850s. There has been some lack of clarity about the details of his first publications. Most accounts, including Spence Watson's, tell us that he published his first volume of poems in 1859, and some say this was in Morpeth, though all agree that no copy is extant. We can, however, clear up the details of Skipsey's first publication in book (or perhaps pamphlet) form, from an article in the *Gateshead Observer*, which appeared in the issue for July 10 1858, p.6, announcing 'The Pitman-Poet'. One assumes it was written by James Clephan, the

16

editor,[2] since it has an educated range of reference, and no fear of comparing a pitman with a peer. It adds useful information about the very earliest attempts of Skipsey to publish, and some lights on his character. It confirms that he had tried a school, which was not a financial success. Since the comments on the book mention that this is a proof copy, the date of the first edition must be near the date of the article. We now know Skipsey was selling it for sixpence, and we have a slightly fuller notion of the title page. The review chooses 'Hey, Robin' as does the *Newcastle Courant* review of two months later, but we get some additional idea of its contents. This is Skipsey's first appearance in the press as a poet, and his description as 'The Pitman Poet' is already attached to him:

THE PITMAN-POET.

THE printers were at our heels, clamorous for "copy;" the hour of publication was nigh at hand; the mail-train was approaching, and must be "saved;" when the door of our office opened, and there stood in the doorway a young man of modest aspect, craving untimely audience, yet in a tone so diffident as to bar refusal. He was a pitman, he said, and wrote verses; and his friends had persuaded him (as friends *will* do) to print them. He had also been advised to seek the aid of the *Gateshead Observer* in bringing his book into notice. And here, having got so far, he produced a copy, with the following titlepage :— "Lyrics. — By J. S., a Coal Miner. — (Woodcut of Durham Cathedral.) — Durham: Printed by George Procter, Marketplace. — 1858." — He added, in answer to one or two questions, that he was not strong, and was anxious to be done with hewing. He had tried a school, but with no great pecuniary success; and would be glad of any congenial employment, It was, so far, the author of "The Pitman's Pay" over again; and may the parallel run on to the end!

When the poet had departed, and we had a few minutes to spare, we took up his "Lyrics," afraid lest we might not be able to speak of them

---

[2] James Thomas Clephan (1804-1888) was born in Monkwearmouth, and became editor of the *Gateshead Observer* from 1838 until his retirement in 1859. He also wrote poetry.

so favourably as, for the author's sake, we could wish. We were agreeably relieved. We found the pitman to be a true poet — a man of decided genius. Timidly, but superfluously, he introduces himself to the public. "This little book," says he, "is the production of a working man — a miner. It is his first flight in the fields of poesy. As the mother-bird gently guards the early essays of her callow brood, and, where they are weak and fluttering, lends them the support of her own stronger wings; so they who have the strength which a liberal education supplies, are entreated to use it, not to crush, but to sustain, a new adventurer in his first timid and uncertain essay.

" 'Sirs, it is well to have a giant's strength,
" 'But '*tis* not well to *use* it as a giant.'" ,

Well said; but "J, S." possesses that which a "liberal education" cannot give — genius; for Nature is impartial in her gifts, conferring them on prince or peasant alike; and he may dismiss all fears as to his reception by cultivated minds.

We pass over "A Patriotic Invocation," (probably inspired by the visit of the illustrious Kossuth to the banks of the Tyne,) and come to "Annie Lee," "fair and sweet to look upon."

"To conceive her step, conceive
"One beating time unto a tune:"

A pretty conceit, and the best lines in the song. — "Hey, Robin," is better throughout; and we give it entire:—

Hey, Robin! jolly Robin! ;
Tell me how thy lady doth?
Is she laughing, is she sobbing?
Of grave or merry mood, or both ;

Is she like the lambkin, skipping
With her servants in the hall?
Or the sour steer under whipping,
Sour to each and sour to all?

Is she like the violet, breathing
Blessings on her native place?
Or the nettle, cankering, scathing
All who dare approach her grace?

18

Is she like the dew-drops, sparkling
When the morn peeps o'er the land?
Or the cloud the heavens darkling, :
Boding tempest near at hand?

Tut! to count the freaks of woman,
Count the pebbles of the seas!
Rob, thy lady's not uncommon,
Be or do she what she please !

Is not that a diamond from the mine? It is not without flaw, certainly;
but a little polish would make it perfect.

We would quote "The Lad o' Bebside" and "The Lass of
Willington Dene," (who may be man and wife, now, for anything that
we know); but we leave them for the perusal of those who apply to
Mr. Procter, "white saxpence" in hand, and turn to

LOVE'S ABSURDITY.

Alackaday! how Love will cavil,
Swearing black is white, till he
Is sentenced by his loving she,
With loving looks, unto the devil.

Not for worlds should Reason teach him
What to think or how to act;
But he'll deny a fact's a fact,
If Beauty's smile doth so beseech him.

Like to the epicure who feedeth
On rich sauces that do tend
To haste him onward to his end,
Wrong'd Nature to him vainly pleadeth ;

Aye ! pleas or threats alike he spurneth,
And with hand most doth take
The bait that leads him to the stake,
And triumphs while the faggot burneth.

The second line of the last verse halts, but the lameness may be the printer's, our copy being a "proof".

Here is a sweet little lyric in a different strain : —

I had a merry bird,
Who sang a merry song;
And you may take't upon my word,
The day it was not long,
In the presence of my bird,
With its merry, merry song.

Did Fortune strew my path
With crosses none might bear
Without a better faith
Than's allotted mortals here,
They would vanish into air
As my birdie wooed my ear.

And thus went things with me,
Until, with silent step,
Death came across the lea,
And laid my bird asleep;
And ever since that hour
I've done nought but sigh and weep.

The pathos of the closing verse is admirable. The second sins against sound faith, which knows of no crosses beyond its consolations.

One more piece — and but one. It shall be "The Violet and the Rose," which reminds us of some of the conceits of our older poets: —

The Violet invited my kiss:
I kiss'd it, and call'd it my bride,
Was ever one shghted like this?
Sigh'd the Rose, as it stood by my side.

My ear ever open to grief,
To comfort the fair one I turned:

20

Of the fickle thou sure art the chief,
Frown'd the Vi'let and pouted and mourn'd.

Then, to end all dispute, I entwined
The love-stricken blossoms in one:
But that instant their beauty declined,
And I wept for the deed I had done. '

Tut! man: — talk not of men of "liberal education," cap in hand. He who can write verses such as these, be he pitman or peer, may never lift his bonnet, otherwise than in courtesy, to the proudest scholar in the land. We ask for our poet, therefore, no commiserating aid. A man so nobly endowed by Heaven — to whom, in his own words, "creation's self is other to that it seems to common sight" — is no fit subject for commiseration, having gifts which should inspire his own deep thankfulness, and the respectful admiration of others. But if, as we hope, there be amongst our readers some good stewards of their substance who would honour themselves by stretching out a helping hand to struggling genius, and lift it from the darksome mine, we shall rejoice to bring them face to face with our pitman-poet —

Who knows that, by dint
Of hard labour and toil,
By the battling with sorrow
And ridicule's smile,
Is the laurel obtain'd
That encrowneth the brow,
And marketh the children
Of Genius below.

That is how the account ends, but there is another review immediately below it which bears on the topic, and deals with an aristocratic poet. This next review begins:

THE POET-PEER
THE Pitman-Poet had gone — our paper had been published — the claims of another week were upon us — when a Poet-Peer looked in upon us: — not, like "J. S.," *in propria personae,* but in the form of a

21

Queen's messenger — a postman — bearing, in striking contrast to the miner's sixpenny "Lyrics," a baronial book of sumptuous print — a lyrical translation by Lord Ravensworth of the Odes of Horace — dedicated to the Prince of Wales, with a graceful eulogy on the classic author as an agreeable teacher of the minor morals of life, if unequal to those higher and graver lessons which the world has learnt from One whose era began when the Roman poet had passed away.

Nature, we have said, (in our notice of the pitman's poems,) is no respecter of persons; and we have here two notable examples of her impartiality. While the miner was turning his verses in the pit-row, the noble coalowner was similarly employed in his castle of Ravensworth, in scenes as fair as those of the Sabine valley where Horace breathed his song. The Roman poet, whose motto was " Eat, drink, and be merry, for to-morrow we die," wove old materials into his epicurean verse ; but his noble translator, poet though he is, uses no such freedoms with his great master. He renders his odes into the English tongue as faithfully as the words of one language may possibly be exchanged for those of another.

Probably following the hint from Clephan, on Friday 17 September 1858, the *Newcastle Courant* (issue 9586. 'Literary Notices') reviewed a book by 'J.S.' which must be the same missing edition, with its Durham publisher. Probably the fact that it bears only the initials 'J.S.' helps to account for its having been so elusive, but the poems quoted are ones which appear in later editions. This is the second notice of Skipsey's work. He was 26 years old.

LYRICS. – By J.S., a Coal Miner. – (*Durham: George Procter.*) – This is a very small book; but it is a genuine one. There is a soul of genius in it; and that is more than can be said of nineteen-twentieths of the books in this world. We have read these poems with interest and delight. We have read them with interest, because they are the production of a working man, a miner; who informs us in his tiny, modest, too modest, preface, that the book is his "first flight into the fields of poesy." We happen to know also, from other sources, that the "coal miner," who here stands before us in the character of poet, has had only the very humblest advantages in respect of education; and it has been therefore with surprise that we have read verses from his pen

which, though they do not reveal that the author has grasped the whole compass of our vernacular, do nevertheless show that he has a remarkably extended vocabulary at his command, and can marshal that vocabulary into effective, and even polished, rhythm. But he has not filled his book with mere verse; it is a book of poetry. To say that it were filled with poetry of the very highest order, were mere flattery. The author's muse aims only at humble flights; and on that very account always rises the more steadily and safely. But that he has the poetic faculty, is undoubted. Coal miner though he be, he is one of Nature's intellectual aristocracy, capable of enjoying and imparting the pure delights of poetry. We will only add that the name and circumstances of the author are known to ourselves; and that any purchaser of his "Lyrics," which may be had for a few pence, will experience not only the delight and interest which we have experienced in their perusal, but will have the additional satisfaction of making the hearth of a working miner in the county of Durham, with wife and family, glow with a light and warmth which his own fireside, however brightly it may blaze, would fail to fling around. We find room for a simple and pleasing specimen of this working pitman's productions: –
[quotes 'Hey Robin' and 'A Word of Good Cheer']

The whole of the poems, it may be added, are wholesome in their moral tone and tendency.

Clephan was obviously not content with simply noticing Skipsey's book of poems. He made sure that Skipsey's name was kept in the minds of Tyneside poetry lovers. The *Gateshead Observer*, which came out weekly on Saturdays (except when Christmas and New Year were Saturdays, when it appeared on the Friday), always featured a type of 'poet's corner' in the top left hand corner of page 6. In the period following the July 10 notice and before Clephan's retirement in 1860, the following poems by Skipsey were used:

Saturday July 24 1858, p.6: 'Death' (From "LYRICS" by JOSEPH SKIPSEY, Coalminer, Gilesgate Moor, published by Procter, Durham), 12 lines beginning 'Death is fearful! Say not so'.

23

Saturday July 31 1858, p.6. 'A Lyric', 4 x 4 line stanzas beginning 'Lo! The Sun begins to rise', signed Joseph Skipsey, Pitman Poet, Gilesgate Moor, Durham, July 29.

Saturday August 7 1858, p.6: 'To a Girl on Hearing Her Sing'. 5 x 4 line stanzas. beginning 'Oh, chant again that theme, sweet girl'. Signed Joseph Skipsey, Pitman Poet, Gilesgate Moor, Durham, Aug 3.

Saturday September 18 1858, p.6: 'Tell Me Not', a sort of triolet with 9 lines and three times the refrain 'Adeline'. Signed Joseph Skipsey, Blaydon September, 1858.

Saturday March 19 1859, p.6: 'To my Child', 7 x 4 line stanzas beginning 'O, my blest child! I call thee blest'.

Saturday May 14 1859, p.6: 'Beauty, Beware!' 5 x 4 line stanzas.

Saturday June 25 1859, p.6: 'The Modest Maid', 3 x 8 line stanzas beginning 'Oh could I a garland braid'.

Interestingly there is a poem from 'Our Rhyming Hewer', in the issue of September 11 1858, but it does not sound like Skipsey. He seems to have taken sole possession of his title as the 'Pitman Poet' very early.

Lyrics obviously did well enough to encourage a reprint and the Newcastle City Library holds two copies of a book whose title page reads: '*Lyrics* by Joseph Skipsey, second edition, published in 1859 by Thomas Pigg & Co., Clayton Street, Newcastle upon Tyne'. It is dedicated to 'Mr. William Reay, Artist.' William Reay (see below) was also a pitman, a painter, and a poet, who emigrated two years later to New South Wales. Reay, whose friendship Skipsey always remembered, had encouraged him to publish, and showed his poems to Archdeacon Prest, who may well have been the person who directed him to Clephan's office.[3]

The style suggests that Clephan was the author of the second review. He was certainly aware of the second edition, which was published just before the Burns centenary celebrations of 1859, and is

---

[3] Edward Prest (1826-1882), from 1851 chaplain and then master of Sherburn Hospital; from 1861 rector of Gateshead; archdeacon of Durham, 1863 until his death on 26 October.

the volume referred to in the following account. On 25 January 1859 there were three main celebrations in Newcastle of the centenary of Burns's birth, (reported in the *Newcastle Courant* of Friday 28 January 1859): a banquet in the Town Hall, a less expensive dinner at the Music Hall, and 'A Nicht wi' Burns' in the Lecture Rooms, which had talks, songs and readings but no food or drink. At this last celebration a vote of thanks was given to the organisers and performers, and then:

> Mr CLEPHAN, editor of the *Gateshead Observer*, in seconding the vote, said, while Mr Gerald Massey was deploring the want of an English poet – a real people's poet – there was at the present time, perhaps in that very room, a person who had written poetry which would not have disgraced even Burns. That person had that very day published a batch of poems which were equal to any in the English language, and yet he was in poverty. Mr Clephan read two or three extracts from the book, which were very well received by the audience. (This allusion by Mr Clephan was to the poems of Joseph Skipsey, a pitman, which were favourably noticed in the *Courant* some time ago. Mr Skipsey is undoubtedly gifted with the poetic faculty; and we trust the poems which he has now given to the world will meet with a considerable sale, being published at a very reasonable price.) Mr Clephan also mentioned that the poet was now without occupation; and he (Mr C.) hoped that some of the gentry of Newcastle might be able to give him employment, so that it might not be said hereafter, that whilst they were celebrating the centenary of a departed poet, they were neglecting the wants of a living son of genius. (Applause.)
>
> The motion, on being put, was carried by acclamation.
>
> Mr BARKAS, in replying, said it struck him, by the appearance of the room, that, after all was paid, such as printing, &c., there would still be a surplus left over, and he thought a fitting opportunity was presented to apply the proceeds to a charitable object. He thought if they were to purchase a number of Mr Skipsey's – (that was the poet's name) – books, and send them to all the mechanics' institutes in the Northern Counties, they would do Mr Skipsey a great service, and it would also benefit the public at the same time. (Mr Barkas here

asked the audience if they were agreeable for the surplus to be so disposed of, and they signified their willingness by great cheering.)

The same events were reported in the *Gateshead Observer* of 29 January 1859 in a slightly different way:

> Mr James Clephan seconded the motion, and said, in allusion to a line in Mr. Hollock's poem, that if we truly believed, in this our day, that Robert Burns was "his country's glory and her shame," we would best evince our sincerity by a more wise and generous treatment of the poets and prophets who were living amongst us. Let us not throw stones at the contemporaries of Burns, and give stones to those who wear his mantle, when they ask for bread. He held in his hand a small book, published that day, being "Lyrics by Joseph Skipsey," a pitman poet, who, without those advantages of education which Burns possessed, had written verses of which Scotland's greatest bard would not have felt ashamed. He trusted it would not be written of us, in an after day, that we had celebrated the Centenary of Burns, and left Joseph Skipsey, whose book saw the light on the same day, to starve. – Mr. Clephan read one or two of Skipsey's lyrics, and expressed a hope that some kind hearer might have the ability, as well as the will, to give the writer employment. – Mr. Barkas, who was called upon by the Chairman to respond, proposed, with his characteristic liberality and good feeling, that the surplus receipts should be applied in the purchase of copies of the "Lyrics," for distribution among the Mechanics' Institutes of the Northern Union – a proposal which was carried with great applause.

Clephan's announcement was not only useful publicity for the books, but it found Skipsey a job as an under-storekeeper at the ironworks of Hawks, Crawshay and Co. in Gateshead, a post he held from 1859 to 1863. On 20 January 1860 his first daughter Elizabeth Ann Pringle Skipsey was born (she was later to marry John Harrison). However, Gateshead did not have happy memories for the Skipseys, since their son William was run over and killed by a train of wagons on the Tyne Main Wagonway in Gateshead on 7

September 1860. The *Newcastle Courant* reported on the 14th of September that

> a little boy, about three years old, named William Skipsey (son of Joseph Skipsey, the "pitman poet"), attempted to get on to the waggon to ride, when he was crushed by the wheel. An inquest was held on Saturday, by Mr Favell, coroner, and the jury returned a verdict of "Accidental death." The coroner, however, admonished the driver to be more careful when he came to the footpath, and to look out to see that no children came on the way.

The 1861 Census shows the family was living at 3 Hawk's Cottages, Gateshead (evidently a works-connected house); he is 29, described as a labourer, born in Chirton, with his wife Sarah (32), born in Norfolk, Watlington (some records wrongly call this Wallington), and children Cuthbert (6), born in Chirton, and Elizabeth (1), born in Bedlington. On 27 April 1862 Harriet Skipsey was born.

Mining is an industry not unused to tragedy, but 1862 was particularly bad, since it saw the Hartley Colliery disaster on 16 January. The breaking of an engine beam caused the blockage of the pit's single shaft (laws were subsequently passed making it compulsory for mines to have two shafts) and led to the death, mostly by suffocation, of 204 men and boys trapped in the pit. There were agonizing days of frantic and finally unsuccessful attempts at rescue, and the unfolding tragedy was followed in the national press. Skipsey responded with his poem 'The Hartley Calamity', a moving ballad of twenty-five stanzas in traditional style, which he read at clubs and meetings to raise funds for the widows and orphans of the tragedy. Robert Spence Watson, who was afterwards Skipsey's staunch supporter, friend and eventually his biographer, was at Hartley when the final news came, and it may well have been at one of the fund-raising occasions that they first met. It was certainly in the early 1860s. In his biography of Skipsey (p. 7) he wrote that 'For forty years we were close friends, and a month seldom passed without our meeting. He was a constant guest at my house, and few events occurred to either of us which were not made known to the other.' Skipsey was a man of great presence, and in quoting 'The Hartley Calamity', Spence Watson says that 'I only wish that I could in any words reproduce the effect which it made when Skipsey himself read it. It was scarcely like reading . . . he entered so evidently into the spirit of the thing and brought out the terrible, tragic nature of the slow death creeping over father and son, carrying away brothers side by side, and told by broken words scratched upon some of the tins, that it was impossible to listen without being greatly affected. The scenes in certain of the places where he read it were almost too painful' (p. 43). Ernest Rhys in *Everyman Remembers* remarked on 'How impressive the old skald looked standing up to declaim this dire death song.'

An early image of Skipsey

28

1862 saw the publication of his *Poems, Songs, and Ballads* (Hamilton & Co., Newcastle upon Tyne), and this reached a wider public, being reviewed (anonymously) by John Westland Marston, in the *Athenaeum* (no. 1822, 27 September 1862, p. 401). Marston had some stern, but useful and accurate things to say about where Skipsey's talents lay. The review is fairly brief, but it was notice in a national paper:

> These poems are led off by the story of Potiphar's Wife done into blank verse – the blandishments of the wanton, perhaps unavoidably, being made far more prominent than the uprightness of the virtuous Hebrew. The legend of Balder is once more treated in the poem that follows. Mr. Skipsey shows some vigour of expression, but he is too often turgid and ambitious. Such phrases as "trial-hatched despair," "the woe-inflicting fire-brands of remorse," "eyes like burnished chandeliers in crystal balls," denote not strength, but inflation, and will certainly be abandoned by Mr. Skipsey should he ever gain the secret of true power.

It was a salutary lesson, and one he seems to have taken to heart.

Skipsey may well have been relieved to put behind him the bad memories of Gateshead when Robert Spence Watson and other friends secured for him a job as assistant librarian at the Newcastle Literary and Philosophical Society in 1863. Unfortunately, he was more interested in the contents of the books than in attending to the needs of the Society's members, and in any case it didn't pay as well as mining, so he returned to the pits. Spence Watson records that he worked in Newsham, Cowpen and Ashington, before settling in Backworth. His son Joseph was born in 1869, although we are not clear where; the 1871 census says Earsdon, the 1881 census says Newsham, the 1901 census Blyth. The second Cuthbert was born in Cowpen in 1872, and the plaque reproduced on p.111 adorned a gift from men who worked under him there. The *Morpeth Herald* for 22 September 1866 offers a possible sidelight on his life when it reports on the first annual exhibition of the Blyth, Cowpen & Newsham

Floral & Horticultural Society, and it may well be our Joseph Skipsey who came second in each of the classes for 12 pods of peas, 2 cauliflowers, and 2 carrots.

The present village of Backworth looks a small and fairly insignificant place, but Spence Watson wrote that 'Backworth has . . . always been a centre of intellectual life', pointing out that it took an active part in taking up opportunities offered by the Cambridge University Extension movement. In 1879, says Spence Watson, in four villages of a total population of 19,000 there were 1,700 students, 'and I much doubt whether in the educational history of the world there has ever been a similar fact' (pp. 49-50).

Skipsey published in 1864 the book whose title page runs: '*The Collier Lad and other Songs and Ballads* by Joseph Skipsey, Author of "The Reign of Gold," and other songs and ballads, Newcastle upon Tyne: printed by J. G. Forster, 81, Clayton Street. 1864.' It contains twenty-one poems (noticeably omitting Potiphar's wife), and culminates in 'The Hartley Calamity'. It looks as if *The Reign of Gold* is another unrecorded book – perhaps a pamphlet – published before *The Collier Lad*, since it is mentioned on the title page, and a flyer at the end of the book announces: '*Shortly to be Re-printed, by Subscription, uniform with "The Collier Lad, and other Songs and Ballads,"* Price Two Shillings, The Reign of Gold, And other Songs and Ballads. By Joseph Skipsey. Subscribers' names will be received by Mr J. G. Forster, Printer and Publisher, 81, Clayton Street, Newcastle-upon-Tyne. March, 1864.' On the verso of this flyer are printed 'OPINIONS OF THE PRESS ON THE REIGN OF GOLD, And other Songs and Ballads' with review comments from the *Edinburgh Daily Review, Newcastle Guardian, North of England Advertiser, London Journal, Newcastle Daily Chronicle, British Controveralist* [*sic*], *Inverness Advertiser, Gateshead Observer, Newcastle Daily Journal,* and the *Stirling Journal.*

Skipsey indicated his affection and his debt to James Clephan when in 1865 he called his son, born on 3 August, James Clephan Skipsey, but the young James lived only five months and died 'from a severe cold' on 16 January 1866. Emma Skipsey was born on 24

January 1867, but in 1868 three of the Skipseys' children died: Cuthbert on 16 October, Emma on 24 October, at the age of 1 year and 9 months, and Harriet on 30 October, in her seventh year. Skipsey wrote in the family bible: 'The children died from Scarlatina. Let me here say that three more lovely and affectionate children were never born into this world. Whose loss has bowed their Parents heads down into the dust, and upon reflection it is my belief that the dear jewels were wrongly treated.' We have no clue as to the nature of this wrong treatment. The family were well supported in their tragic loss: The *Morpeth Herald* reported on 7th November, 1868 that

> The friends of Mr. Joseph Skipsey, the well-known lyric poet, will learn with regret of the heavy bereavement he has sustained in the loss of three of his children, all within the short period of eleven days. On Sunday week, his eldest son, aged 14 years, was interred, and was followed to the grave by the most of the workmen of Newsham Colliery, and since then his two daughters, aged respectively two and six years, have also died.

Perhaps as a result of these deaths, he and Sarah Ann Fendley finally got married at the parish church in Tynemouth on 21 December 1868. They were living at Low Chirton. On 27 September 1869 a son, Joseph Skipsey, was born (he later married Sarah Leech and had 3 daughters). Not long after the wedding they moved again, and the 1871 Census shows them at Newsham: Joseph Skipsey (38), coal miner, with his wife Sarah (42), with two children, Elizabeth (11), born in Bedlington, and Joseph (1), born in Earsdon. They have a boarder, John Hagan (22), a miner born in Norfolk at Holt. The Norfolk origin suggests a possible family connection with Sarah.

In 1871 Skipsey's *Poems* were published by William Alder at Blyth. In 1872 Joseph and Sarah had their last child, a son, Cuthbert Skipsey, who was born on 14 June 1872 (on 21 July 1900 he married Julia Crawford – born on 7 April 1873; they had one daughter, Violet Celia, and a son, Joseph Fendley Skipsey, who was the father of Roger J. Skipsey).

At about this time (1872) Skipsey appears to have been drawn into some political activity. Whereas he remained opposed to violent action, he seems to have been willing to assist in achieving a negotiated settlement. On 20th July, 1872, the *Morpeth Herald* reports on two meetings with the coalowners. The first involved a delegation of miners, including Thomas Burt, while the second was with a deputation representing the colliery deputies which 'consisted of Mr. Joseph Skipsey, of Newsham, and Mr. James Campbell, of Sleekburn'. After the meeting, the deputation reported back to their colleagues:

> The gathering took place in the large hall of the Mechanics' Institute, Newcastle, and there was a large attendance of delegates from the different collieries of the county. – Mr. Skipsey, in commencing the proceedings, said it would be remembered that at their Blyth meeting on the 10th of June a series of resolutions had been drawn up with the view of explaining their wants to the coalowners. As they had now got a reply, however, he proposed to read these resolutions over, in order to let all present see how far they had been complied with:-
>
> "1. – That no deputy work more than six shifts per week, except in cases of emergency, and then these latter to be paid at the rate of one day and half for one day's work.
>
> "2. – That each deputy receive 5s 6d per shift, and also advance of 10 per cent. on the drawing of timber; but in places where there is no drawing, that they receive 6s per day.
>
> "3. – That each deputy have the privilege of travelling the air courses at least once every three months.
>
> "4. – That each deputy receive 10s per week smart money in case of accident occuring [*sic*] in the mine which shall render him unable to follow his employment"
>
> Now, the whole of these matters had been considered by the coalowners that morning, and they had at once come to the conclusion to grant the 5s 6d per day – (hear, hear, and applause) – although they added that they could not see their way to giving 6s in places where there was no drawing. The members of the deputation, between themselves, only considered this latter as a minor matter,

because, even if the masters had consented to pay them 6s when there was no drawing, they could always have managed to evade the law by just providing as much of that kind of work as would keep them clear of the extra charge. The resolution, unfortunately, does not say how much or how little drawing they ought to have before being entitled to the 6s, and hence if the owners chose to give them drawing which would only amount to one penny above their 5s 6d, they could have no further claim upon them. This was an error, and it would be for the men hereafter to consider whether or not it was worth rectifying. (Applause.) With regard to the travelling of the air courses, he was glad to say that that had been unhesitatingly granted; while the 10s smart money was readily conceded to them also. (Hear, hear, and applause) The greatest difficulty with which they had to contend was with their references to extra shifts, as the owners could not see their way to doing without overtime. They assured the men, however, that there should be no shifts run when it could possibly be avoided, and that, as shooting stone and other things were objected to, all shifts required of them should be confined to deputy work. (Applause.) The masters objected to the payment of time and half, but said they would not object to pay at the rate of 6s for all extra shifts. It would thus be seen, at least he thought so for one, that the men had achieved a decided victory, for with the exception of overtime – and even that was not entirely refused – the masters had consented to every request made to them. The required 10 per cent on the price of drawing was strenuously opposed by owners on the ground that such work already cost sufficient. Still, he considered that the result of the interview had been most gratifying, and the victory must seem all the greater when it was remembered that the coalowners had only met the hewers half way. Mr. Campbell and himself had been invited to join the deputation from the general body of miners; but as they had no commission so to act, they resolved not to join with them, and he was disposed to think that that resolve had worked for the better. If they had joined with the hewers, undoubtedly 10 per cent. would have been all that would have been offered to any of them. Instead of that, however, and thanks to the soundness of their case, somewhat more than 20 per cent. had been secured. (Loud applause.) – Mr. Campbell was decidedly of the opinion that although the 10 per cent. on drawing had been refused, the masters had conceded the 6s per day where there was no drawing; and further he had understood that should any man work an extra shift at any time, for each extra shift he would also be paid the 6s. The masters had at first stumbled at the request for paying 6s to those men who had no drawing, and requested the deputation to retire in order that it might re-considered; but on their again entering the room, the masters said they had come to the conclusion to grant the desired advance under the circumstances indicated. (Applause.)

His work as a negotiator did not mean that he relaxed his output as a poet. The title page of Skipsey's 1878 volume reads: 'A Book of Miscellaneous Lyrics, by Joseph Skipsey, author of "Annie Lee," "Two Hazel Eyes," "Meg Goldlocks," "My Merry Bird," "The Fairies Adieu," and other ditties; Bedlington, printed for the author by George Richardson.' It was this book which introduced him to Dante Gabriel Rossetti, through the good offices of Thomas Dixon (1831-80), the Sunderland cork-cutter to whom Ruskin's letters published as *Time and Tide, by Weare and Tyne* (1867) were written, and who had become a passionate supporter of Skipsey's work. Dixon worked tirelessly to develop the artistic and educational facilities in his native town, and corresponded, generously and sometimes irritatingly, with many writers of the day. Ruskin's *Time and Tide, by Weare and Tyne* considered Dixon the 'highest type of working man'. It is very likely that Dixon, who wished to be in contact with the writers and intellects of his age, approached Skipsey, probably in 1878, when the correspondence between the two men begins.[4] In a letter to Dixon from 20 Percy Street, Backworth, on September 26, 1878, Skipsey writes:

> Dear Sir, Accept my heartfelt thanks for the interest & the trouble you have exhibited & subjected yourself to on behalf of one who was till so very recently a complete stranger to you.

---

[4] The collection of letters from Skipsey to Dixon is currently in the possession of Simon Marshall, of the Stone Gallery, Burford, who has graciously allowed us to quote from them.

He is clearly introducing himself to Dixon, summarising his life story and providing a list of respected local acquaintances:

> I am or was known to the Venerable Archdeacon Prest – to G.B. Forster Esq. M.E. under whom I worked at the Newsham & Cowpen Collieries about ten years – to H. Richardson Esq. M.E. under whom I have worked nearly five years – to G. Crawshay Esq. under whom I served as sub-storekeeper at the Gateshead Iron Works nearly four years – to R. S. Watson Esq. of Newcastle-upon-Tyne to whom I have been personally known fourteen years & to Mr James Clephan late Editor of the Gateshead Observer to whom I have been known some nineteen years.[5]

He goes on to describe his present situation:

> I am working under the Mr Richardson above named at the Backworth Collieries. My position is that of a Master Shifter – that is an officer whose duty it is to get during the night the mine put into a working order for the day workers – Apropo[s] to your inquiry as to my prospects – I can only say that I [am] without any at [least] of a cheering nature & that I shall die as I have lived a coalminer.

The final paragraph of the letter shows that Dixon has already introduced Skipsey's book to Rossetti, an introduction which, as we shall see, elicited a letter from Rossetti:

> In conclusion let me say that I am delighted to think that you have introduced my book to the notice of the celebrated Rosetti [sic]. I am fully aware of the many defects & imperfections of the work but I have also a hope that he will meet with some things that may merit his commendation. I shall surely feel happy if he does so.

---

[5] This tallies with the date of their meeting at the *Gateshead Observer*.

Skipsey was becoming used to giving his life story and provided an informative Preface to the *Miscellaneous Poems* (1878), which he used again in *A Book of Lyrics* (1881):

PARTLY from deference to the opinion of a few well-wishers, and partly from an impression that it would be proper so to do, I beg leave to state that the author of the following Lyrics is a coal-miner, and that he was sent into the coal pits of Percy Main, near North Shields, to help to earn his bread while yet a mere child, and when the sum total of his learning consisted in his ability to read his A.B.C., or at most his A. B. ab card. When it is stated that the requirements of the times at that period necessitated the young to be in the mines from twelve to fourteen hours per day, it will be seen that they had little leisure for self-culture, and that only by dint of perseverance, and by not allowing the few spare moments to remain unutilized that should present themselves, could those who had a desire, acquire anything in the shape of education. The author being possessed with the requisite aspiration, soon had felt what is thus expressed, and instead of spending his hours on the play-ground, he devoted his Sundays and other holidays to the acquisition of the ability to read, and to decipher simple arithmetical questions. These operations were usually performed in his mother's garret, (he had no father — the father having lost his life when the writer was a baby "in arms") whilst he learned himself to write with a piece of chalk on his trap-door — a door connected with the ventilation of the mine, and which it was his duty to attend. In this rude way were his studies pursued, and with what success may be indicated by the fact, that before he was eleven years old, he had formed the romantic notion of trying to commit the Bible to memory, and that he had actually acquired a number of the chapters by "heart," and was only prevented from proceeding further by the ridicule of a grey-bearded wiseacre to whom he had had the temerity to disclose his project. By the time he was sixteen years old, he had from a Lindley Murray which had been presented to him by an aunt, and through much effort and perseverance, acquired a knowledge of the elements of English Grammar. Other studies chiefly of a scientific nature succeeded this — then that of poetry — or rather the poetry of celebrated poets, as Shakspere, Milton, and Burns, for otherwise the love of the muses had grown up with him from his infancy, and he had actually practised verse-making, while he was yet a child behind his trap-door.

After the elapse of a few more years, and after making repeated efforts and in vain to get a suitable situation out of the mines, he printed a batch of lyrics (1859), which earned him the respect of several eminent persons in the North of England. Through the kindness of one of these he was placed into the office of sub-store-keeper at The Gateshead Iron Works. This was at the commencement of the year 1859, and at the latter part of the year 1863 he was placed, on the commendation of the same kind friend, as sub-librarian to the Literary and Philosophical Society, Newcastle-upon-Tyne. This latter office, which was certainly extremely congenial to his tastes, he only held a few months , when from the inadequacy of the income to meet his domestic needs he was necessitated to give it up, again to find himself a toiler in the coal mines. In 1871 he again resorted to the printer, and issued a small volume of poems, which obtained a kindly notice not only from the *Newcastle Chronicle* and the rest of the local papers, but also from many of the London weeklies, including the *Literary World* and the *Sunday Times*, and also a kind word from the *Athenæum* and the *Spectator*; whilst several of the pieces included in this issue were honoured by a translation into the French tongue and published in the *Beautés de la Poësie Anglaise par le Chevalier De Chatelain*. The encouragement thus received has helped to stimulate the author to persevere in his attempts at self-culture, and the embodiment, when the impulse has come upon him, of his sentiments and feelings in verse, until he finds himself in possession of material for the present book—a book which he now submits to the public in the hope that it may at once prove of some interest to the peruser, and be the means of rendering some little personal benefit to himself.

In conclusion, the author would say, that should the present venture, several of the Pieces of which have already seen the light, find favour with the public, it may in due time be succeeded by a companion volume — a book of Songs and Ditties, and in the two brochures thus offered, would be comprised nearly the whole of his verse that the author would care to put into print.

JOSEPH SKIPSEY, *Backworth*. August, 1878.

The 1881 edition adds the footnote: 'As in this re-issue, a selection of these effusions has been inserted to supply the places of several pieces on speculative subjects, which the author has deemed it advisable to omit, the work Songs and Ditties is not now contemplated, – J.S.'

Encouraged by Dixon's contact with Rossetti, Skipsey must have introduced himself to the poet, and Rossetti responded on 29 October 1878 (the letter is addressed to Skipsey at 20 Percy Street, Backworth, Northumberland, and posted on the 30th):

> 16 Cheyne Walk / Chelsea / 29 Oct: 1878
> My dear Sir
> I much esteem such a letter as you have written me. I believe I may now safely tell you (as I wrote to Mr Dixon yesterday) that a friend of mine – a very influential critic – is engaged on a review of your Lyrics which will appear in the Athenaeum – I suppose either this week or next. It will not be a mere notice, but an article of fair length. I believe I may now state this as a certainty, & hope heartily that your book may benefit as it deserves.
> I am gratified to know that my poems appeal at all to you. Yours struck me at once. The real-life pieces are more sustained and decided than almost anything of the same class that I know – I mean in poetry coming really from a poet of the people who describes what he knows and mixes in. "Bereaved" is perhaps the poem which most unites poetic form with deep pathos. The Hartley ballad is equal in another way, but written I fancy to be really sung like the old ballads. "Thistle & Nettle" shows the most varied power of all perhaps. In this & throughout the book, the want I feel is of artistic finish only, not of artistic tendency: the light touch sometimes seems to come to you most happily of its own accord, but when not thus coming, it remains as a want. Stanzas similarly rhymed are apt to follow each other, & the metre is sometimes often filled out by catching up a word in repetition, — I mean as for instance at page 100 —
> "May be, as they have been, may be" &c
> Other favourites of mine are "Persecuted", "Willy to Lily", "Mother Wept", (this very striking) & "Nanny to Bessy". It seems to

me that, as regards style, you might take the verbal perfection of your admirable stanzas "Get Up!" as an example to yourself, & try never to fall short of this standard, where not a word is lost or wanting. This little piece seems to me equal to anything in the language for direct & quiet pathetic force. "The Violet & the Rose" I think very perfect, & a singular instance of exact resemblance to a charming class of Blake's work. I greatly admire the image evolved in the stanzas on page 25.

Among the poems of aspiration, the one which appears to me greatly the finest in expression & value is "The Soul's Hereafter." Few could speak on such a subject with such unhesitating justice of view.

I am glad indeed if any word of appreciation on my part can give you pleasure, but would not advise you to use such in a public way, on account of the malignity of literary cabals. I am conscientious in saying this.

I do trust that this book may succeed so as to improve your position permanently. This of course is not to be done in a moment as no one will feel better than one so clear-headed as yourself, but it may be a firm first step to that end.

With best wishes for the welfare of you and those dear to you,
I am yours sincerely
D G Rossetti

> (*Newcastle University Robinson Library:*
> *Spence Watson Collection*, SW 1/16/44).

The review by the 'influential critic', who turns out to be Theodore Watts, duly appeared in the *Athenaeum* for 16 November 1878, and gave warm praise to the new book amid its rather woolly criticism:

> It is easy to distinguish real poetry from specious poetry as it is easy to distinguish a real daisy from an artificial one. Mr. Skipsey, who is – or until lately was – a pitman of Percy Main, near North Shields, has written a volume of undoubtedly genuine poetry. All genuine poetry, however multitudinous in its varieties, is ultimately divisible into these two kinds: that which, under the conditions of art, truly reveals the poet's soul; and that which, under the conditions of art, truly

paints the external world. The soul revealed may be as healthy as Chaucer's or as unhealthy as that of Petronius Arbiter; and the external world depicted may be as lovely a world as Chaucer's England, or as foul a world as Neronian Rome; but its reflex – so absolutely vital is truth – may, in proper hands, become poetry. And those few who can faithfully reveal or faithfully paint are of the same brotherhood – whether they be Juvenals or Tennysons; just as the mulberry and the upas are – say the botanists – of the same species, notwithstanding that from the one we draw poisonous death, from the other mulberry wine.

If the poet will only ask himself before he begins to write, whether he has the rarest of all gifts, the gift of speaking the truth – whether he can truly tell what he truly feels, or truly depict what he truly sees, he will be spared that waste of force which wrecks so many lives. Most likely he has not this gift. However, Mr. Skipsey has it or he could not have written thus: –

> On, on they toil; with heat they broil,
>   And streams of sweat still glue
> The stour unto their skins, till they
>   Are black as that they hew.

Again, listen to the stern "collect" of the pitman's working day: –
[quotes "Get up"]

This is the way to write of everything; but, in a general way, the modern poet is just the man who cannot do it. He must be fine; he must be flowery: his eye must roll "in fine frenzy." If he had seen the "Douglas die," he would have been the last man in that fray who could have told us: –

> The Persé leanéd on his brand,
>   And saw the Douglas dee;
> He took the dead man by the hand,
>   And said, "Wae's me for thee."

Yet it is obvious that he who can tell us neither what he sees nor what he feels should do anything rather than write poetry. Not that he need be discouraged however; the man who cannot write a sonnet

40

may, very likely, be able to amass a fortune or govern a country. Instead of wasting his energies, for instance, upon "Revolutionary Epics" and tragedies about Don Carlos, let him turn to something else – to party politics, and it is quite surprising what he may achieve.

Great personal interest attaches to this volume. There is a fundamental difference between the personal outpourings of the mere lyrist and poetry which is purely objective. Between them there are many suggestive distinctions, none, perhaps, being more notable than this, that while in the latter case the only question that can without impertinence be asked concerning the poet's work, is simply Is it good? In the former it is legitimate to inquire (within decent bounds), Under what conditions was the work produced? A poem addressed to "Mary in Heaven" may be beautiful; but, if it is known that the Mary apostrophized was a real Mary, and that the poem came straight from the heart of a bereaved poet, what before was interesting becomes a most precious possession for the human race. Again, if Edgar Poe's greed for "fame" had been a little less, – if he would have permitted his readers to remain in the delusion that the 'Raven' was the outcome of his own personal passion and remorse, instead of a clever piece of mechanical ingenuity, that which now amazes us by its cleverness would have placed him in the highest rank of lyric poets.

And so with regard to Mr. Skipsey's volume: unequal as it is, – full of imperfect workmanship and of mannerisms which surprise the reader at first and vex him at last, – it yet gives evidence of so masculine an intellect and so true an insight that its claim to attention cannot be passed by. But when his preface tells the conditions under which the poems were produced, – and when he brings before us the picture of a little unclad child spending its life, not in meadows and leafy lanes, but in a coal pit, its life and limb depending upon its vigilance in opening and shutting a trap-door for the coal trucks to pass through, and when he proves to us by his work that this little thing is one of the lost children of Paradise endowed with the gift of song, a rich pathos is shed over every line. This is how he begins his preface: –

[quotes a large portion of Skipsey's Preface]

Poetry written under such conditions as these – if true – must be new.

41

Wherever there is true observation of human life there is certainly humour. Mr. Skipsey's humour is tender and playful.

The rest of the review consists in telling the story of 'Thistle and Nettle' and quoting thirteen of its stanzas, Watts concludes that 'This is charming, and the volume contains other poems in the same vein.'

Skipsey's correspondence with Dixon lasted until Dixon's death in 1880. In the last letter, Skipsey is still trying to finalise arrangements for their trip to London. Much of the correspondence deals with relatively mundane matters, but there are some insights into Skipsey's thinking. In December 1878, he comments that:

> ...the Athenaeum Review has undoubtedly helped to draw some attention to the book but as yet that is not much felt in the way of sale. The reason of this I imagine to be the want of a central Pub[lisher] . . . who could have sent out copies to the various booksellers.

He also criticises the balance of the reviews, in the process revealing a confidence in the quality of his writing:

> as yet none of our Reviewers – not even the Athenaeum – has given one in which the philosophical poems which occupy full one half of the book, should have justice done them. Of course some of these are colored [sic] by unpopular ethics to which it would be dangerous to refer but surely one of the questions for a critic to decide is whether a poem is written with ability & if so I would ask if the pieces entitled The Mystic Lyre, Omega, Music, Love without Hope, The Question, The Angel Mother, The Inner Conflict, The Hell Broth, The Reign of Gold, the Downfall of Mammon &c have not the true lyric ring what poems in the English tongue have it? I know that self praise is no commendation but I also know that if a poet or an artist be proficient in his art he must be conscious of it. Indeed what is it but this consciousness which enables a Wordsworth a Blake and a W. B. Scott to spend their lives in obscurity, poverty, or subject to the calumny & obloquy of a world who is ever ready to bow the knee

to the idols of Fashion while their by-many-degrees inferiors in poetics & artistic worth are riding the gilded car of wealth and notoriety? Without this consciousness we could have no originality in poetry or art & with this the original poet can afford to wait.

He continues to have reservations about the critics, writing in December 1878:

> The critique in the Chronicle is the best that has yet appeared on my poems. The writer however misses his mark in his strictures on Willy to Lily. He seems to overlook the circumstance that the feeling pourtrayed [sic] in the latter part of the poem is that which might [be] termed "First-love" that wherein the tender passion first takes possession of the young heart & so colors [sic] his imagination that the object of his affections as seen therein assumes the appearance of an angelic being.

By January 1879 he is addressing Dixon as "My Dear Friend", writing:

> I thank you from the bottom of my heart for the interest you have subjected yourself to on my behalf. Had I only met with a friend like yourself a few years ago I feel I should have occupied a much different social position than I now do.

He provides some information about when some of the poems (interestingly referred to as 'songs') were written:

> Two of my best songs – "Hey Robin" & "The Lad of Bebside" were written while I was working as a common miner at Pemberton Colliery. I also produced "The Violet & Rose" & a rough sketch of "Thistle & Nettle".

Some of the correspondence relates to art exhibitions which Skipsey visited on Dixon's recommendation. Skipsey found Rossetti's Penelope 'displayed the same weird power which characterises his ballad-poems' but found Lilith 'too crowded with details'. Millais'

'The Romans Leaving Britain' as 'a wonderful production' but 'his "Child October" had no charms for me & the subject of "Jepthah [*sic*] & His Daughter" is too painful for me to think about'. As for Turner, he 'may be one of those geniuses whose products require intense study before they can be properly understood & appreciated'. Despite his earlier comments, he was also delighted by a statue of 'Jepthah & Daughter' by Westmacott which displayed "all the poetry in the subject".

Dixon continued to promote Skipsey's poems, and Skipsey wrote in May, 1880 that he was 'glad that you still have hope of disposing of a few more copies of Lyrics. I herewith forward you twenty copies by mail'. The correspondence continues in June:

> I need not add that I am delighted to think that you have secured a couple of London Book-sellers to my Lyrics, or that I feel grateful for your proposal to advertise in the Athenaeum. As to a form of advertising I think I cannot do better than cut you out the one which Mr Lewin is inserting [in] his excellent magazine with a few additional words which you can mend or mar as you deem best.

By June 1880, Skipsey is making arrangements to go to London, at Dixon's invitation:

> It so happens that the cheap trip train falls upon a day when I have to commence the measurement of our stone bargain men's yardage – a piece of business that occupied me for two days & after I accomplish this I have the Colliery Shift Bill to make out & submit to the inspection of the manager. This is done upon the Saturday. I have acquainted our manager however with your kind proposal and he says after the Saturday I could take a few days liberty.
>
> I should certainly feel a great pleasure in visiting the famous Town in your company. And then to have the honour of shaking hands with some of our living great men in Literature & Art!!

No doubt encouraged by the contact with Rossetti, in 1880 Skipsey took this trip to London with Dixon, who perhaps thought this would be his last chance to introduce Skipsey to his metropolitan friends. On the way they rather surprisingly stayed with Professor Jowett, Master of Balliol. While in London they met Burne Jones, Holman Hunt, Theodore Watts, and Rossetti. Rossetti reported his meeting with Skipsey to his friend Hall Caine:

> The other evening I had the pleasant experience of meeting one to whom I have for about 2 years looked with interest as a poet of the native rustic kind, but often of quite a superior order. I don't know if you noticed somewhere about the date referred to, in the *Athenaeum*, a review of *Poems* by Joseph Skipsey. The review was written by Theod: Watts, to whom I had the pleasure of introducing the book — sent to myself by an excellent fellow in the North who spends his life in spreading the knowledge of what is worthy. Skipsey has exquisite – though, as in all such cases (except of course Burns's), not equal powers in several directions, but his pictures of humble life are the best. He is a working miner, and describes rustic loves and sports and the perils of pit-life with great charm, having a quiet humour too when needed. His more ambitious pieces have solid merit of feeling, but are much less artistic. The other night, as I say, he came here, and I found him a stalwart son of toil and every inch a gentleman. In cast of face he recalls Tennyson somewhat, though more bronzed and brawned. He is as sweet and gentle as a woman in manner, and recited some beautiful things of his own with a special freshness to which one is quite unaccustomed.
>
> (*Dear Mr. Rossetti: The Letters of Dante Gabriel Rossetti and Hall Caine 1878-1881*, ed. Vivien Allen (Sheffield, 2000), pp.123-4).

Georgiana Burne-Jones, in her *Memorials of Edward Burne-Jones* (2 vols, Macmillan, London, 1904, vol II, pp.107-9) recalls that summer and the impression it left on both her and her husband:

> This summer brought us a brief friendship and then took away the friend it gave — Mr. Thomas Dixon of Sunderland, to whom Ruskin wrote the letters afterwards published as Time and Tide by Wear and Tyne. Mr. Dixon had already written to Edward, but first came to the Grange one day early in June, when he lunched with us.

45

We felt the delicacy of his nature, and liked him at once; and the liking was quickened when we found that his great wish was, not to introduce himself, but to bring his chief friend and hero, Joseph Skipsey, up from Newcastle to London for a few days, in order to make him known to some of the men whose work he specially honoured and who he thought would recognize Skipsey's gifts. What he said of his friend is now well known: that he had worked in a coalpit from the time he was seven years old, but that a ray of the divine light of genius had lit up even that black world for him, and by this time he was a man to be worshipped by at least one other — who was telling us the story.

A few days after this, Mr. Dixon dined with us to meet Morris, and my diary says it was "a good evening," but details are lost. The Sunday following is clearer in memory; it was a beautiful summer day and the two friends came to the Grange together, and we all walked and talked together in the garden before supper. Skipsey was a noble-looking man, with extremely gentle and courteous manners. Edward talked much with him and was struck by his wide knowledge of English literature and his poetic vision, but felt that the circumstances of his life had left him at a disadvantage in the art of writing poetry for which nothing could make up. He felt also that one so sensitive in nature must see this clearly, and must carry about with him the pain of knowing that all he did could only be judged after allowance made. Thinking of this, Edward wrote sadly, yet hopefully: "Of course his poems are not much to us; only one measures by relation, and sometimes the little that a man does who has had no chance whatever seems greater than the accomplished work of luckier men — on the widow's mite system of arithmetic, which is a lovely one."

Twice again the friends lunched with us during the week they remained in London, and the last time was farewell for this world to Mr. Dixon, who went back to Sunderland, took to his bed, and in little more than a fortnight sank and died of exhaustion following on the excitement and exultation of carrying out his generous plan.

The thought of Skipsey working in a dark mine whilst he himself painted pictures by daylight was intolerable to Edward, who was not comforted till things were altered, and the poet and his wife had obtained the post of caretakers of Shakespeare's house at Stratford-on-Avon.

Not long after their visit, and after the unhappy death of Thomas Dixon, Edward Burne-Jones sent a letter to Skipsey informing him that a friend of his (who turned out to be Gladstone) was interested in his work and would like to offer an annuity of £10 with which to buy books. Skipsey's scrapbook preserves the letter from E. W. Hamilton, dated the fourth and postmarked 5 October 1880 from 10 Downing Street, which says: 'Sir. I have the pleasure to inform you that Mr. Gladstone has directed that an annuity of £10 should be paid to you out of the Royal Charity Fund, as from the 1st May last. The requisite form to enable you to obtain the money will be sent to you by the Paymaster General; and on future occasions, you should apply direct to the Paymaster General, Whitehall, London.' An article in the *Times* of 19 October 1880 reported that 'Joseph Skipsey, a Northumberland miner, author of several lyric poems, and now residing at Backworth Colliery, near Newcastle, has received an intimation from Mr. Gladstone's private secretary that, in consideration of his literary services, the Queen has been pleased to award him an annual pension.' This was reported also in the *Liverpool Mercury* of 18 Oct 1880 and in the *Newcastle Courant* for 22 Oct 1880.

A number of letters from Burne-Jones to Gladstone's daughter Mary fill in the background to Burne-Jones's efforts, and also indicate his rather patronising view of Skipsey's poems; but, whatever his attitude to the poetry, his attitude to the man is extremely practical. The following extracts from his letters are from *Some Hawarden Letters 1878-1913 written to Mrs. Drew (Miss Mary Gladstone) before and after her marriage*, chosen and arranged by Lisle March-Phillipps and Bertram Christian (Nesbit & Co, London, 1917). The letters must come from 1880, and they tell their own story:

I have posted Mr. Skipsey's book and put inside it a photograph which is very like him, because the perky lithograph in front of his

47

poems would give you a wrong impression of a head that is leonine and dignified. Don't read the poems as literature but look at them as rather wonders to have been written at all in such dark surroundings. I send also his letter to me, in spite of things about me that will make you laugh, because all helps to build up an imagination of a very exceptional character. How many more are there, I wonder, one knows nothing of?

But if some lightening of his life could happen for him – literally lightening – so that he might not live so much in the dark . . . (p. 82)

. . . Only he is a very real man and would be unable to do anything but work and work hard for his living; but if books could be more accessible – he is very anti-materialist, as you see, but now his friend is gone will be unhelped and alone, and my little offer of friendship is too far off for much comfort, and too unsubstantial in spite of all he may wish to feel about it. But perhaps somewhere in the North a librarian might be wanted – no sinecure, for I know his honesty and reality would shrink from it – but some real work that might help him to develop a soul that has had nothing yet to help it but its own self. I know I felt very much abashed before him, thinking how terrible the pit life must have been from infancy to a nature so sensitive and imaginative, and I could not bear to watch him look at my pictures, for the look of his face had the same kind of pain in it that seeing a starved creature eat hungrily would have. (p.83)

. . . my pitman has written, having had a bad vision that I was ill which touched me. We will try to get him to upper earth some day. People did once get him a librarian's post of some little kind, but they paid so little to him that he was obliged to go back into the earth to get food for his wife and babies (p.84).

. . . I have been thinking over your kind proposition. He is not in need of money; his hard work keeps him and his children. It is leisure to read, not books, that is wanting. I send him books, but he cannot read them – has literally no time – it is hard work in the pit and then the body tired out, and sleep, and more pit, and so on always. No sunlight (better than all books), no summer, no history of the year, but darkness always. There is never in his letters any least complaint, not in all my talks with him has he, more than a memorable once, said how happy he could be above ground. I remember it the more

48

because he did not din it into one's ears but said it once very quietly. I will tell him of it if you think it is best for him to choose.

. . . Please is it a permanent fund of one hundred a year or does it end if the country wants to be Tory? I only want to know because of the wording of my letter, not that it would otherwise make any difference, for he is so simple that if he liked to take money at all five pounds would be the same as a hundred (pp. 84-5).

. . . I sent the tidings to Mr. Skipsey that it was for life, for I had cautioned him before that it might only be for a few years – and he is prettily overpowered and bids me thank his unknown friend. So you were right, and it was a blessed idea of yours and has ended beautifully – and his letter is written in a state of great happiness, and saying that he can educate his two boys with it – nine and eleven they are. He is gratified and happy about it in the childish degree one likes people to be in.

The details of the arrangements are lost, but the picture of Skipsey here is a touching one.

At this time an article on 'A Miner Poet' appeared, in *Capital and Labour: an Economic and Financial Journal*, no. 349, Oct 27 1880, price 4d. It enthusiastically, though not uncritically, welcomed his latest book as an example of what a working man's efforts could achieve. The following week's issue saw a response from R. S. Watson, the Newcastle solicitor, whose praise of Skipsey began with the simple comment: 'He is probably the most remarkable man I have met with'.

At the time of the 1881 Census, Skipsey's mother Isabella (82) was still living in Chirton at 17 Middle Row, with her widowed daughter Hannah Robson (59), and two boarders. Both the women are said to have been born in Percy Main. Joseph Skipsey (49), Coal Miner, is living not far away in 20 Northumberland Terrace, Backworth with Sarah (52), son Joseph (11), who was born in Newsham, and Cuthbert (8), born in Cowpen. Also living there at that time is Jane A. Graham, a grandniece, aged 6 and born in North Shields. In that year Skipsey brought out *A Book of Lyrics, Songs, Ballads, and Chants*, New edition, revised (London, David Bogue).

In 1882 Skipsey left Backworth for a post which his friends had found for him and his wife as caretakers at a Board School in Mill Lane, Newcastle (later referred to as the Bentinck School). On Tuesday 6 February 1883, Spence Watson proposed Skipsey as an honorary member of the Newcastle Literary and Philosophical Society, and he was duly elected; the letter and the envelope postmarked February 7 1883 are in Skipsey's scrapbooks. Skipsey also delivered a lecture at the Literary and Philosophical Society on 'The Poet as Seer and Singer', which was subsequently printed in a journal, cuttings from which are in his scrapbook. It is a romantic version of the nature of the poet, claiming that he sees 'the hidden beauty of things, from which he lifts the veil', and, although the picture is rather overdone for modern taste, one can gather a little of the rhetorical force of the man. The idea of the poet takes shape from references to Emerson, Shelley, Plato, Swedenborg, Jamblichus, and allusions to Shakespeare, Blake, Collins, Burns, Milton, Spenser and the Ballad writers, as if Skipsey is trying to state his credentials to write about poetry. Once or twice one gets a glimpse of the pitman poet: 'The poet who would sing his thoughts into the hearts and souls of his fellow-men must to some extent live the lives of these men, and must essentially have a deep sympathy with whatever concerns their highest weal', he writes, and the poet, 'though he is born with the golden bell in his soul he may not be born with the silver spoon in his mouth'. He was obviously becoming used to lecturing, since the *Newcastle Courant* announced on April 20 that speakers including Joseph Skipsey would give talks to the Tyneside Students' Association.

He was beginning to gain confidence and reputation as a literary figure and was making useful contacts in and around Newcastle. On 7 July 1884, the *Leeds Mercury* reported that Walter Scott, the Newcastle publisher, was 'preparing an edition of English and American poets, to be issued in monthly volumes, under the editorship of Mr Joseph Skipsey, a North-country writer of local verse.' This was to be the 'Canterbury Poets' series, and Skipsey was to edit and introduce selections of William Blake (June, 1884), Samuel Taylor Coleridge (July, 1884), Shelley (August, 1884), Edgar Allan Poe (October, 1884), Robert Burns (two volumes, dated April, 1885). Reviewers of these editions had varied views about the introductions, and the introductions themselves are of varied quality, not really surprising in volumes published at that rate.

Ernest Rhys, the future editor of 'Everyman's Library', had trained as a mining engineer in Durham. (At the time he spelled his name Rees, which was his father's preference, and the spelling under which Ernest P. Rees gained his election to the Institute of Mining and Mechanical Engineers on 4 March 1876 while he was attached to Langley Park Colliery, and his manager's certificate of competency and of service on 16 September 1882 in Durham). Rhys wrote with reference to Skipsey that he 'must have first met him in the North, at Newcastle-on-Tyne, the mining metropolis, early in the eighties. He looked the skald, tall, with stalwart shoulders, too tall for a pitman, with grizzled dark hair and beard, and the deepest of deep-set black eyes under shaggy eyebrows. His speech was rough Northumbrian, not easy for a southerner to follow, and he read or recited his verses with kindling force, very affecting to hear. A version he had written of the old song, *Willie comes not from the Fair*, was, as he said or intoned it, a haunting thing'. Rhys went on to recall (in his *Everyman Remembers*, Dent, 1931, p. 224ff.) how Skipsey was one of the sources of 'Everyman's Library':

> Turning over some old letters, half afraid of what they might disclose, I came on one signed D. G. Rossetti and addressed to a poet unknown to most of you to-day, He counted to me, however, as a later skald in my mining days, and his name, Joseph Skipsey, must not be forgotten. My real debt cannot be counted, for without him and his love for his fellow poets I might never have become poet-mad, or ended by shouldering a thousand authors.

Rhys acknowledged his debt to Skipsey more specifically when he added that

The sequel to the story of Skipsey's brief career as editor is in a degree the introduction to mine, as my first book was the volume of George Herbert's *Poems* he asked me to edit for him.

It was about this time that Skipsey's friendship with William Reay was resumed (if it had ever been interrupted) and reinforced, though they were never to meet again in the flesh. Reay had been the dedicatee of Skipsey's early work, but had emigrated to Australia in 1861, and it is worth a digression on Reay to explain some of Skipsey's later verse. William Reay, miner, artist, emigrant to Australia, art teacher, poet, was born in 1830 in Newcastle upon Tyne and died at Waratah, New South Wales in 1903. His obituary says that he studied art under William Bell Scott (1811-1890) and Henry Hetherington Emmerson (1831-95), which is not unlikely. Scott, who became head of the School of Design in Newcastle upon Tyne in 1843, saw his job as a 'way of discovering talent among the working-class men' (*ODNB*), and Emmerson was a local boy, an ex-pupil of the School of Design and the painter of *Reading the Queen's Letter* (1862), a picture which he studied from life after the Hartley disaster. The obituary also says that Reay practised as a painter in various parts of England, though we have no evidence to say where. We can say however that he, his wife Mary Jane, née Watson, and their young son Robert, emigrated to New South Wales aboard the *Queen Bee*, as part of a group of nearly 300 mainly Irish emigrants, departing from Plymouth on 28 December 1860 and arriving in Sydney on 31 March 1861.

Some accounts say that Reay went to Australia in response to the success there of his painting *Adam and Eve Expelled from Paradise* which toured to Newcastle, Maitland and Sydney (the picture has not been located); others say he was a late participant in the gold rush; and it could be said that he went to avoid the oppression he felt in England. Certainly the subject of his painting reflects his concern with being forced out of paradise, and he lived out its theme of exile. He discovered, however, that no artistic patronage awaited him, and ironically found work as a coal-miner in Newcastle, New South

52

Wales. But he did eventually receive a commission to paint the portrait of Governor Sir John Young (later Lord Lisgar), for which purpose he was granted several sittings at Government House. When the portrait was displayed at a dinner given in the governor's honour by the Hunter River Valley Vineyard Association in 1868, Sir John said (as reported by the *Maitland Mercury*) that he believed that Reay was a self-taught artist and that 'It appears that Reay is a working coal miner by trade, but, having a natural talent for drawing, has contrived in his leisure hours to attain a very creditable proficiency in the art. Some time ago, Mr. Reay instituted a portrait club amongst his fellow miners; he painted their portraits ... they remunerating him by certain weekly subscriptions. Some of these portraits were seen by Mr. Keene [the manager], who, struck by their fidelity and the talent displayed in their execution, mentioned the circumstance to Sir John Young, and at the same time requested his Excellency to encourage this self-taught genius by having his portrait taken'. In spite of the unqualified praise of Sir John and Lady Young as to the portrait's fidelity, Reay returned to the mines, and the *Mercury* concluded, in phrases reminiscent of Skipsey's case, that: 'It is a great pity that so much promising talent should be buried in obscurity'. Reprinted in the *Sydney Morning Herald* on 29 May 1868, the story led to commissions from Mayor Walter Renny and other public men of Sydney, the novelty of being a painter-miner proving Reay's major asset. When his oil painting, *View of Waratah Colliery*, was lent to the 1870 Sydney Intercolonial Exhibition by D. N. Joubert, Reay was wrongly catalogued as 'W. Bray', though the fact that he was identified as a miner at the Waratah Colliery confirms that the painting was indeed his.

At this stage Reay's reputation was more likely to be boosted by stories of native working-class genius than by his professional training. Like Skipsey, he was a miner for his bread and butter and an artist by inclination, picking up instruction as he could find it. When he became an art teacher, his claims to training came more to the fore. He became art master at Newcastle Grammar School for nineteen years and visiting art teacher at Miss Dowling's Young Ladies Seminary in West Maitland and at Mr Theobald's Collegiate School, thus being responsible for the art education of a great number of children in the Hunter Valley. He also painted portraits of local residents such as Mr and Mrs Hannay (recorded in the 1880s) and/or a pair of unidentified sitters (Mitchell Library, State Library of New South Wales, Sydney). His large oil painting of a bushranging incident was purchased by a Newcastle police officer.

In the early 1880s, Reay, who had published a number of his poems in the Australian *Newcastle Herald and Advocate*, was encouraged by his friends to put together a volume of poetry. This duly appeared in 1886 as *Poems and Lyrics* by William Reay, Artist (E. Tipper, West Maitland, 1886), and its 'Author's Preface' gives useful detail about Skipsey at this time. Reay tells us that, before he published the poems, 'I thought it best to submit them to some acknowledged authority, and get an opinion as to their merit.' He duly sent them back to England to ask what Skipsey thought of them. The preface makes great play of Skipsey's eminent position 'among the Sons of Song of that mighty land', of the translation of his poems into French and German, of his Civil List annuity, and of his editions of the Canterbury Poets, and proudly quotes Skipsey's comments on Reay's verse, which reflect much of what had been said of his own verse and state clearly his views on verse making:

"Your poems are delightful and display a great poetical genius. 'The Meeting' is worthy of Burns, and 'The Motherless Foal' is a master-piece. The power which you possess over the peculiar stanza in which you enshrine so many of your poetic fancies, feelings, and sentiments, appears to me to be unexcelled by Burns. I have tried this stanza, but have failed to satisfy myself. From you this form of verse is always natural and easy, and accordingly delightful. It flows from you as freely and delightfully as the stream that sparkles in the light of the morning. All the rest of your poems are characterized by a freshness and sweetness which are not to be found among the products of the polished writers of the age; which age, I may add, is noted for polish both in literature and painting, but little of the qualities which are dearest to the human heart, and which will serve to interest when the studies of the false are neglected. We as rarely as possible meet with those touches of nature from the pen or pencil 'which make the whole world akin.' Your great breadth and depth of sympathy for nature, and especially human nature, has proved your salvation in this respect. I am particularly pleased with the sweetness, airiness and melody of your song 'May Morning.' It is a gush of song worthy of our greatest poets. You will understand what I mean, when I say that it has the Shakspeare quality in it. The longer I live and the more I study the subject the more I am convinced that nature ought to pervade poetry. Your songs, as I have said, are full of nature.

JOSEPH SKIPSEY.

The remarks were endorsed by the editor of the local paper; and the book itself bears out Skipsey's view. The *Dictionary of Australian Artists Online* (from which helpful source much of this account of Reay derives) comments on the archaic language and stereoptypical forms, but the poems have more characteristically an entertaining vivacity and colloquial swing, which almost certainly derives from a careful reading of Burns and perhaps of Skipsey himself. 'The Lass of Brownieburn' and 'Peggy is Unkind to me' would not be out of place in Skipsey's volumes. Several of the poems are in the Burns-like stanza which Skipsey so liked, and which he imitated. Reay's verse 'Epistle to Joseph Skipsey' (pp. 51-55 of his book and see pp. 166-71 below) is in this form and Skipsey's replies gain a good deal from Reay's example. And the serio-comic 'To a Motherless Foal' and his apostrophe 'To a Mosquito' have a pleasant humour. In this last poem, by the way, there are lines that indicate that part of the reason for his emigration was 'To seek for gold and sunny skies.'

In old age Reay was respected as Newcastle's 'painter-poet' and the painter-miner was forgotten. He has an understandable nostalgia for the country of his birth, and describes his exile as a 'banishment', but in his 'prize poem' hymning 'Australia, or the Land We Live In', he recognizes that he left England because 'the hand of oppression was lifted so high, / And blighted each hope and compelled us to fly; / We burst every bond for we wished to be free'. Australia gave him that freedom to succeed in his chosen arts. He died at Waratah in May 1903, leaving a wife, four sons and two daughters.

In January of 1886 Skipsey received a donation from the Royal Bounty of £50, and his annuity was raised to £25 a year. It was in that year also that Skipsey went on holiday in the Lake District with Spence Watson, who reports the 'wonder and delight' of the man who had never had a real holiday and had not seen such mountains before. His poem 'The Rydal Trip' addressed to William Reay, which was printed as a broadside for private circulation and of which there is a copy in his scrapbook, deals with the excursion of 'last year'.

Walter Scott, the publisher of the 'Canterbury Poets' brought out Skipsey's *Carols from the Coalfields* in 1886, with a biographical sketch by Robert Spence Watson; the book was praised by Oscar Wilde, who compared the poems to Blake. Wilde's review in the *Pall Mall Gazette* for 1 February 1887, goes over familiar ground but adds his appreciation of the work:

> For more than forty years of his life he laboured in 'the coal-dark underground,' and is now the caretaker of a Board-school in Newcastle-upon-Tyne. As for the qualities of his poetry, they are its directness and its natural grace. He has an intellectual as well as a metrical affinity with Blake, and possesses something of Blake's marvellous power of making simple things seem strange to us, and strange things seem simple. How delightful, for instance, is this little poem: [quotes 'Get up!' the caller calls, 'Get up!' and 'The wind comes from the west to-night'].

He also admits that 'Mr Skipsey's work is extremely unequal, but when it is at its best it is full of sweetness and strength; and though he has carefully studied the artistic capabilities of language, he never makes his form formal by over-polishing.'

It could well have been Wilde's review which triggered the interest of that avant-garde periodical of the late 1880s, *The Century*

Guild Hobby Horse (continued as the *Hobby Horse*). There the most discriminating of critics, Herbert Percy Horne, noticed Skipsey's latest book in the issue of April 1887 in an article headed 'Nescio Quae Nugarum' (roughly translated as 'a few random jottings'). Although he, like Wilde, was critical of some of the poorer poems in the book and felt that it needed pruning, he opened his comments with the remark that 'Of the many volumes of verse lately published, one of the few worthy of regard is that containing Mr. Skipsey's collected poems' (*Century Guild Hobby Horse*, 1.6, April 1887, pp. 76-78). When Skipsey revised the book as *Carols, Songs, and Ballads*, very much on the lines that the review suggested, an anonymous critic in the *Hobby Horse* (perhaps Horne again) wrote that 'In the present day it does not often fall to the good fortune of the critic to be allowed to notice a book comparatively little known, which possesses that most precious of all literary qualities, distinction. Yet, in Mr. Skipsey's book, distinction assuredly there is, and it is to be hoped his work will early meet with that recognition which is the due of every true poet' ('Notes on Some Recent Books', *Hobby Horse*, 3.16, October, 1889, p. 164). A poem of Skipsey's duly appeared in the journal in 1891: 'A Remembrance', two stanzas in his familiar style, was published in the same issue as the first appearance of that most sensational of Decadent poems, Ernest Dowson's 'Non sum qualis eram bonae sub regno Cynarae' (*Hobby Horse*, 5.22, April 1891, p.60).

There is a brief sidelight on Skipsey's career as caretaker of the Bentinck Board School in Elswick in a report in the *Newcastle Weekly Courant* of Friday 13 January 1888. It records the theft of '20 head of poultry, value £2 10s, from a shed adjoining Bentinck Board Schools on the 11th inst., the property of Joseph Skipsey. – Mrs Skipsey, wife of the prosecutor, said on Wednesday night she saw the poultry securely locked up in the shed next to her house.' Two men, James Carruthers and William Rowe, were arrested and committed to trial, where they were convicted to nine months and four months imprisonment respectively.

At this time, Walter Scott published a new edition of his poems, called *Carols, Songs and Ballads* (1888) which was widely reviewed, as for example in the *Birmingham Daily Post*, which opened with the striking comment that 'Work of such poetic quality as that which this volume contains is not likely for long to be dependent for recognition on any interest attaching to the personal history of the author, and yet under no conceivable conditions, while human nature remains what it is, will that personal history fail to give an added charm to what is in itself so fine and true.' It ends its first paragraph by calling him 'this remarkable man'. The review ends with an accurate description of the poems: 'All through – though occasionally the verses will not rank high as poetry – what is written comes directly from a man's heart and life: they have strong individual character, and are not the mocking-bird's tune learned by heart. They have what so much of excellent verse produced in our day lacks – the note of distinction. Grave or gay, pathetic or humorous, amorous or tragic, they are full of simplicity and strength, are manly and original, and have the charm – of which the full perfection is found nowhere perhaps but in Burns – of perfect spontaneity.'

Also in 1888 William Andrews of Hull included Skipsey in his *North-country Poets* (London, Manchester and Hull, 1888, pp. 61-5), and sent a newspaper cutting, which described Skipsey as 'genial and gifted' and a 'warm-hearted man', and obviously spoke from experience when he said his 'manners are most agreeable, his conversation pleasing – he is in short one of nature's noblemen.' Skipsey is represented by three poems, 'Mother Wept', 'The Violet and the Rose' and 'The Reign of Gold', and the biographical introduction is written by Andrew James Symington. Yet another of Skipsey's many contacts, Symington ends his brief note with the comment that 'Mr. Skipsey having been introduced to me by Mrs. G. Linnaeus Banks, some eighteen years ago, having corresponded with me at intervals ever since, and having recently visited me, I need only add that I quite agree with Dr. Watson's high estimate of one who is truly a remarkable man.' The *Newcastle Weekly Courant* for Friday 27 July 1888 reported of Andrews' book that 'The introduction to each author is so fresh and agreeable that we feel certain a more extended acquaintance will be desired by the reader.'

But as the Bentinck School grew, the duties became too much for the Skipseys, and in September 1888 Skipsey was found a place (one assumes by Spence Watson) as porter in the Durham College of Science, Newcastle upon Tyne, whose Armstrong Building (the centre of the future Newcastle University) had recently been opened. Spence Watson's account points up the irony of the situation. Skipsey had fulfilled the post admirably, but:

> this too proved clearly not the place for him. One morning I was taking Lord Carlisle over the new building, and our Principal joined us (Principal Garnett). As we went along the great corridor, Skipsey, bending beneath the weight of two coal-scuttles of considerable dimensions, met us. He at once pulled up, and Lord Carlisle, recognising him, took him by the hand, and said, "My dear Skipsey, whatever are you doing here?" We had a long talk, and explanations were made, but I saw from that time that it was quite impossible to have a College where the scientific men came to see the Principal and the artistic and literary men came to see the porter (pp.71-2).

A solution seemed to offer itself in the anticipated vacancy at the Shakespeare Birthplace in Stratford upon Avon. The minutes of the Shakespeare Birthplace Trust Executive for May 6 1889 give the details of the post that would be advertised:

> Custodians wanted for Shakespeare's Birthplace. A married couple without children or two ladies, to take charge of the building and attend to visitors. Hours on week days from 9 A.M. to 7 P.M. in summer, and until dusk in winter, and for two hours on Sundays if required, during which times one will be expected to be always in attendance and both if necessary.
>
> They will be required to live in the adjoining house and will have Rent, Rates, Coal, Gas & Water free with a joint Salary of £100 a year. They will be subject to the instructions of the Committee and the

engagement may be terminated on three months notice from either side.

Written applications to be addressed to The Chairman of the Committee, Shakespeare's Birthplace, Stratford on Avon, before Friday May 24th 1889.

(*SBT Collections* TR2/1/1)

The minutes continue by noting that a 'long discussion took place as to the question of Salary & eventually the two sums of £80 & £100 were voted upon. Five voted for £80 and six for £100.' There were 132 applications for the post, and Richard Savage, Secretary to the Trustees, recorded in his diary that he was 'busy all day acknowledging receipt of applications and answering enquiries' (*SBT Collections* ER82/6/5) over a period of several days. The applicants were narrowed down first to 25 and then to 6, who were to be approached. The first to be interviewed were the Misses Harper and Beaumont, of Leamington, on Saturday June 15. The Skipseys travelled down on June 18th, were shown around by Richard Savage on 19th and interviewed on 20th.

Skipsey's candidacy had been supported by Browning, Tennyson, Swinburne, Dante Gabriel Rossetti, W. M. Rossetti, William Morris, Austin Dobson, Theodore Watts, Sir Frederick Leighton, Oscar Wilde, Dr Furnivall, Ernest Rhys, Edmund Gosse, Andrew Lang, Henry Irving, Wilson Barrett, Edward Burne-Jones, Lord Ronald Gower, Lord Ravensworth [reviewed alongside Skipsey back in 1858], Earl Compton, Lord Carlisle, Bram Stoker, John Morley, Thomas Burt, Professor Dowden and others.

Copies of many of the letters of recommendation are in Skipsey's scrapbook. Skipsey was interviewed for the post in Stratford by an august committee who felt, in Spence Watson's words 'the true magnetism of the man', but one interviewer was worried about his pronunciation. Skipsey replied to him that 'I should like, sir, to argue that question. I know that my pronunciation is not quite like yours, but I must be allowed to say that I conceive it is much better, and should like to prove it' (*Joseph Skipsey*, p. 73). He was not asked to do

60

so, but he was appointed. The news was widely reported (*Newcastle Daily Leader*, 8 June 1889).

There is no detail of the interviews of any other candidates. At a special meeting of the executive on June 24:

> Proposed by the Chairman, seconded by Alderman Cox and carried unanimously. That Mr & Mrs Skipsey of Newcastle upon Tyne be appointed Custodians of Shakespeare's Birthplace, according to the terms stated in the advertisement except that no Gas be allowed or permitted in the Custodian's house.
>
> (*SBT Collections* TR2/1/1)

Skipsey felt he had found a kindred spirit in Richard Savage, to whom he wrote on June 25, 1889, accepting the offer of the post:

> P.S. I am convinced that our tastes & aspirations are so much akin that we cannot very well but harmonise & get pleasantly on together. I am not afraid that any misunderstandings should arise between us but should such a thing occur let us exercise forbearance & charity the one towards the other & I have no doubt the appearant [*sic*] wrong will soon right itself & we will gradually be taught by experience the more & more to respect & love each other.
>
> J.S.
>
> (*SBT Collections* ER82/4/1/198)

On his departure from the north, his 'artistic, literary and poetic friends' met at the Liberal Club in Pilgrim Street, Newcastle, to honour him and wish him God speed (*The Newcastle Daily Leader* for 1 July lists the great and the good of Newcastle, including the manager of the publisher Walter Scott). The report of this celebration and farewell in the *Newcastle Daily Chronicle* of 1 July 1889 calls him 'their distinguished townsman' and said that Skipsey was 'eminent for character no less than capacity'. In his address Skipsey outlined his life story and paid tribute to the late James Clephan.

Skipsey's fame had spread throughout Britain, but it was to reach America at about this time. A cutting in his scrapbook is annotated

61

'Louise Chandler Moulton – In Boston Herald – Sunday Aust 18.' On the next page is a sheet of two sonnets by William Ordway Partridge and Louise Chandler Moulton from the *Boston Evening Transcript* of 2 April 1887; the page is annotated to Skipsey with the author's compliments from Partridge, who says he may 'speak for Mrs Moulton also' and it is dated 'Apl. 20 91'. The article is a London letter dated 3 August 1889 and can be dated by its reference to the fact that Skipsey 'has recently been appointed custodian of Shakespeare's birthplace.'

He must have become used to telling his life story, since it appears in almost every account of him, but the most detailed version (though it does contain one or two inaccuracies – like his age when his father was killed) appears in an interview in the *Pall Mall Gazette* for 11 July 1889, just as he was taking up the post in Stratford, and it seems worth quoting it all to indicate what picture of Skipsey was being given to the public at that time.

A POET FROM THE MINES.

AN INTERVIEW WITH JOSEPH SKIPSEY.

I passed through the old pit village of Percy Main on my way to visit Joseph Skipsey, at Newcastle. It is now a pit village no longer, but a populous suburb of North Shields, inhabited by railway men, and "trimmers" from the docks, and workmen from the shipbuilding yards. There is one row of pit cottages still remaining —houses with perhaps two rooms and a garret, with a long slope of brown-tiled roof, and with small, trimly kept gardens in the rear. In one or other of these cottages was born Mr. Thomas Burt, the member of Parliament for the borough of Morpeth, and Mr Joseph Skipsey, miner and poet, who before this article appears in print will have been duly installed as the custodian of Shakspeare's birthplace.

Mr. Skipsey is a well-built, kindly-looking, grave-eyed man, with a head reminding one first of Tennyson and then of Dante Rossetti. A true Northumbrian, one who has seen little of the world outside his native county, Mr. Skipsey's speech has scarcely a trace of that famous "burr" which both Mr. Burt and Mr. Joseph Cowen have failed to conquer.

MR. JOSEPH SKIPSEY.

Illustration to the Pall Mall Gazette *interview of 11 July 1889*

"I want you to tell me," I said to him, "all about your early life, and your means of education, and how you were led to the writing of verse." — "I had no means of education to speak of," Mr. Skipsey replied. "I was born on St. Patrick's Day, 1832. Before I was seven years of age there was a colliery strike, accompanied by rioting. My father was one of the leading men among the miners, and endeavoured to make peace between the rioters and the constables. While he was in the act of speaking to a policeman he was shot dead, and my mother was left with eight children, of whom I was the youngest. Then I went into the mines. I was only seven years of age, but even such little weekly sum as I could earn was of importance to a family like ours. I became a trapper boy — that is to say, I sat all day by a door used for the ventilation of one of the passages of the mine, opening it and closing it as the trams and rollies went through. That was when I taught myself to write. Mostly I sat in the darkness of the mine, but sometimes I had a piece of candle, which I stuck against the wall with a bit of clay. At such happy seasons I amused myself by drawing figures upon the trap-door and by trying to write words. I had learned the alphabet, and the a, b, ab, before going to the pit. I learned to read on Sundays. This was not at Sunday school, but in our own garret. My mother was too poor to buy Sunday clothes for me, and 1 didn't like to go out without them, so I sat in the garret and read. I found a few books of my father's there. There was the Bible, of course, and at ten yean of age I must have known it all through. That was my schooling, then; learning to read in the garret and to write on the trapdoor in the pit."

"And how was your love of poetry awakened?" — "In those days I didn't know that there was such a thing as poetry; but the elder boys in the pit, the putter lads, as they were called, had a habit of ballad singing. It was seldom that they knew a ballad all through, but they used to sing snatches of ballads and songs at their work, and these fastened themselves in my memory. Their incompleteness dissatisfied me, I wanted them all, and as I could not obtain them, I used to fill them out here and there, and piece the fragments together, and so give them a completeness of my own. This patching of old ballads was my first effort at verse-making."

"And the next step?" — "Well, the next step was the composition of new words to the old tunes. 1 do not doubt at this day that the lilt of the old ballads has given a tone to whatever music my verse may be supposed to possess. There was, I think, more love for ancient ballad poetry in those days than there is now."

"But you have been a great reader. When did you make your way to more books than were to be found in the garret?" — "In my fifteenth year I found that an uncle of mine had a small library. I borrowed 'Paradise Lost.' They laughed at me when I took it away. 'Why, Joe,' said my aunt, 'thoo'l nivvor be able to understand that.'

'Well,' I said, 'I mean to try.' The book was a new revelation to me, I was entranced by it. I thought of nothing else night or day, and I believe I accepted the book as a narrative of fact. My enthusiasm induced my uncle to open his whole book-case to me. In this way I came across Pope's 'Iliad' and Lindley Murray's Grammar. The grammar was a great service to one in my situation, as you may believe."

"But how did you come to feel your grammatical deficiencies?" — "I don't believe that I did feel them. One can scarcely explain these things; it is too far off now; but I must have convinced myself that there was a right way of writing and a wrong one, and that this grammar was intended to teach the right way. It somehow seemed necessary to learn."

"And when your uncle's books were exhausted how did you get more?" "I had made the acquaintance of a man named Turner, a bookseller in Newcastle, One day he said, 'Joe, did you ever read Shakspeare?' I had never heard of him, and 'Paradise Lost' I had read more as a fact than as a work of art. Turner pressed Shakspeare upon me. He had a copy, for which he wanted five shillings. I was then seventeen. All my earnings were given to my mother, except a shilling a fortnight. I saved up for ten weeks, and then took Shakspeare home. The book altered the aspect of the world to me. Whole passages rang in my mind. I used to recite them to the other lads in the pit, and I was half crazed for the stage, though I had never so much as seen a theatre."

"And in what order did you read Shakspeare's plays?" "I began with the 'Tempest' and read right through. I think the comedies and histories fascinated me most. It was from Shakspeare that I obtained my chief knowledge of English history. In fact I may almost say that now. [sic] There was another work that was very useful to me, in a different way. Chambers' 'Information for the People' was coming out in penny numbers, that suited my pocket very well, and I bought the whole set. I bought Joyce's 'Scientific Dialogues' too, and the works of Thomas Dick, the Christian Philosopher,' and Chalmers's 'Political Economy.' Chalmers enlarged my views on questions of wages and labour. He steadied my mind, made me weigh matters carefully, gave me a dislike to strikes, and so kept me out of the movements of that time. There were then no such men among the miners as Thomas Burt and William Crawford. I knew Mr. Burt as a boy. We were at Seaton Delaval together. We were never very intimate, for I had no great intimacies; but though he was younger than myself I respected him greatly, and I think that he liked me."

"And to come back to your writing and reading, Mr. Skipsey." — "Well, at twenty I came across Emerson's 'Essays,' and this was another great awakening and sustaining force. Just before this I began to note down some of the verses that I had made. And here I ought to explain that I never wrote anything with a view to publication. I made verses because it seemed a natural and was a delightful thing to do. Sometimes a thing would be months in shaping itself in my mind. I would write it out when I got the opportunity. But I never sat down with any deliberate intention of writing poetry. Writing was merely a transcription of what had taken shape already. Many of my smaller pieces were composed as I was walking to the pit, and some of these have been praised as among the best that I have written. At twenty-one I found that I had as many pieces as would make a book, but after reading them over I put almost the whole of them into the fire. Three or four songs were saved, and are now to be found in my books. I have been told that they were worth saving. One of them greatly took Dante Rossetti's fancy afterwards."

"Did you read your verses to your mates in the pit?" — "No; I had just one friend, now a well-known artist in Australia. One day he said to me, 'Joe, I am going to take some of these verses away.' He took them to Archdeacon Prest, at Gateshead, who asked if there were any more, and wished to see the author. He was the first educated man I had met. The verses were brought out in a small pamphlet shortly afterwards. The late James Clephan wrote a long article about them, and this made me known to the public. Somebody asked one of the men at the pit if he had known that I made rhymes. No, he said, he had worked beside me ten years, and he knew nothing about it; but he knew I was a good hewer."

"You were constantly at work, I suppose?" —"I used to go down the pit at four in the morning. We sometimes came up at four in the afternoon, but more frequently at six. In winter we never saw daylight except on the Sundays. That may be the reason why my verses do not contain more descriptions of natural scenery. When 1 saw the outer world I usually saw the skies with the stars in them."

"But you did leave the pit for a while?" — "Yes. After I had published my second book of verses, in 1873, I was offered employment at the Gateshead Iron Works, and I accepted it. Still later I became assistant librarian to the Newcastle Literary and Philosophical Society; but, unfortunately, what I earned was not sufficient for the maintenance of my family, and I again went back to the mine. I became deputy-overman, and then master-shifter. This last was a position of great responsibility, for it was part of my duty to see that the mine was in a state of safety. My 'Book of Lyrics' was published in 1878. This attracted Dante Rossetti's notice, and he wrote to me, asking me to go up to London. Theodore Watts reviewed the book very favourably in the *Athenaeum*, and when I did visit Rossetti I found that I had already a great number of friends, with William Morris, and Burne-Jones, and William Bell Scott among them. Rossetti was very kind, and it was to me that his very last letter was written. There is little more that I need tell you, except of my delight in becoming the custodian of Shakspeare's birthplace. The secretary, Mr. Savage, and myself, hope to make some discoveries. Mr. Savage has found — what do you suppose? — the name of Nicholas Bottom in an old Stratford register. I wonder what Mr. Donnelly would make of that!" and here Mr. Skipsey, with a pleased light on his face, fell to dreaming of Stratford and of Shakspeare. The duties of the new post will not be altogether strange to him. For some years he and Mrs. Skipsey, a bright, pleasant woman, gentle-looking, were caretakers at a Board school in Newcastle, and more recently they have occupied similar positions at the new College of Science, in the same city. These are strange uses to which to put a poet. Even King Admetus did better to him who "stretched some chords, and drew music that made men's bosoms swell." And what did King Admetus?

—Well pleased with being soothed
　　Into a sweet half-sleep,
Three times his kingly beard he smoothed,
　　And made him viceroy o'er his sheep.

Other newspapers like the *Leeds Mercury* for July made grateful reference to this article, while the *Birmingham Weekly Mercury* for 20 July 1889 quoted the piece almost verbatim. *Reynolds' Newspaper* of 30 June 1889 reported that in the previous year there had been 17,000 paying visitors to Shakespeare's birthplace. The *Northern Echo* of 15 July 1889 wrote of Skipsey's 'merry, active little wife' and commented that 'I wouldn't be surprised to learn that even Stratford is reckoned as having an added attraction by the importation of the worthy Northumbrian pair.' The 1891 Census shows Joseph Skipsey (59), custodian, living at 17 Henley Street, Stratford upon Avon, with Sarah (62), and Lucy M. A. Preston, a 17 year old domestic servant.

Skipsey was much appreciated as the custodian of Shakespeare's house, as this extract from the *Stratford-upon-Avon Herald*, 14th August, 1891, makes clear (the Quotation is placed next to his portrait in the Shakespeare Birthplace Museum):

> Mr Skipsey has been the delight of American visitors and of all who wish to know something about Shakespeare ... the Intellectual portion of the users, knowing his great literary ability, always considered themselves fortunate if they could obtain a few minutes' chat with him.

But the couple's tenure of the post lasted only two years as Skipsey began to find more and more that he was being expected to market what he considered a fraud. His official letter of resignation, dated July 11 1891, reads:

> To the Trustees & Guardians of Shakespeare's Birthplace & Museum
> Gentlemen,
> I most respectfully intimate on behalf of my wife and myself, you would kindly accept our resignation on the Custodianship of the Birthplace & Museum on the 31st of ~~September~~ October next. In thus resigning I may add that we are doing so simply from the fact that we find the duties of the post injurious to our health and particularly so to that of Mrs Skipsey's [*sic*]. I hardly need say that we sincerely regret that we should feel such a change necessary; and that we feel we owe the Trustees, & Guardians our very best thanks for the

kindness & courtesy we have continued to receive at their hands during the more than two years we have had the honour to hold the situation.
I remain
Gentlemen
Your humble & obedient servant
Joseph Skipsey   (*SBT Collections* 93.2)

Skipsey originally asked to leave at the end of September, but when it was pointed out that the terms of his contract required three months' notice, he altered the date to October 31. Charles Flower, Chair of the Trustees, wrote to Skipsey on August 7 hoping he might change his mind:

> ... for my own part, I hope that we may find that some arrangement can be found, by which you at any rate may continue in a post for which I consider you are particularly well fitted, and have given such satisfaction.
>
> (*SBT Collections* ER82/4/4/3/1)

The *Pall Mall Gazette*, which seemed to take a great interest in Skipsey, reported on the problems in its issue of 10 August 1891 and gives a slightly fuller story:

> A DAY IN SHAKSPEARE'S COUNTRY.
>
> "A day of unadulterated pleasure," writes a correspondent, "would have been my description of the latest 'Saturday in Shakspeare's country,' except for one circumstance. This was the communication of the intelligence that Mr. Skipsey had just felt compelled to resign his position as curator of the museum at Shakspeare's birthplace. The pitman-poet of Northumberland is being driven from the post, not merely by the maddening monotony of his daily task as showman of exhibits whose interest rests for the main part solely upon tradition, but also, and perhaps principally, by the senseless jests and brutal behaviour of the many thousands of loutish, and sometimes absolutely drunken, folk whom cheap excursions bring from the big towns of the surrounding district during the summer season. The number of visitors has increased at the rate of ten thousand per annum during the past two years, and the total number last year was

22,000. In the words of one who can speak with authority, 'Mr. Skipsey's sensitive heart has been rent by the Black-Country barbarities which have come under his notice in his capacity of custodian, and as he is anxious to preserve his deep reverence for Shakespeare, his sad heart has dictated absolute resignation of the post he has held for the past two or three years. It is not surprising to hear that, under the circumstances, it is little that Mr. Skipsey has been able to add to the volume of his poetic contributions. But when he gets comfortably settled north again, there is good reason to hope that his muse will be as fruitful as of yore (p. 6).

Sarah Skipsey photographed in Stratford

The Skipseys were replaced by Annie Beaumont and Alice Maud Harper, unsuccessful interviewees of two years earlier.

The events had interesting repercussions. In 1903 Henry James published a story called 'The Birthplace', based on something he had heard from Lady Trevelyan in 1901. Though of a famous Northumbrian family, she had a house very near to Stratford and must have known something of what had gone on. The story is, as one might expect from James, perceptive about the problems of being the curator of artefacts in whose authenticity one didn't believe, and one is tempted to wonder exactly how much James knew about Skipsey's tenure of the post, for, though he knew the general shape of the story, his details do not coincide with what we know of Skipsey and his wife, either in their character or in the facts of their lives. They were hardly 'strenuous and superior people'. Ernest Rhys felt that the story was not one of James's best and that the 'hero is not the least bit like Skipsey, who suffered extremely in the post. He could not dissemble and play the showman's part for the American tourist, or produce a hair of the Great Cham out of his waistcoat pocket. At times he was even rude to the inquisitive tormentors who put silly questions.' James knew that he was embroidering on a hint and seemed not to wish to know more details. This extract from Henry James's notebooks suggests what he did and did not know:

Lamb House, June 12th, 1901.
The other day at Welcombe (May 30th or 31st) the Trevelyans, or rather Lady T., spoke of the odd case of the couple who had formerly (before the present incumbents) been for a couple of years – or a few – the people in charge of the Shakespeare house – the Birthplace – which struck me as possibly a little donnée. They were rather strenuous and superior people from Newcastle, who had embraced the situation with joy, thinking to find it just the thing for them and full of interest, dignity, an appeal to all their culture and refinement, etc. But what happened was that at the end of 6 months they grew sick and desperate from finding it – finding their office – the sort of

71

thing that I suppose it is: full of humbug, full of lies and superstition imposed upon them by the great body of visitors, who want the positive impressive story about every object, every feature of the house, every dubious thing – the simplified, unscrupulous, gulpable, tale. They found themselves too 'refined', too critical for this – the public wouldn't have criticism (of legend, tradition, probability, improbability) at any price – and they ended by contracting a fierce intellectual and moral disgust for the way they had to meet the public. That is all the anecdote gives – except that after a while they could stand it no longer, and threw up the position. There may be something in it – something more, I mean, than the mere facts. I seem to see them – for there is no catastrophe in a simple resignation of the post, turned somehow, by the experience, into strange sceptics, iconoclasts, positive negationists. They are forced over to the opposite extreme and become rank enemies not only of the legend, but of the historic donnée itself. Say they end by denying Shakespeare – say they do it on the spot itself – one day – in the presence of a big, gaping, admiring batch. Then they must go. – THAT seems to be arrangeable, workable – for 6000 words. In fact, nothing more would be – nothing less simple. It's that or nothing., And told impersonally, as an anecdote of them only – not, that is, by my usual narrator-observer – an inevitable much more copious way. (*The Complete Notebooks of Henry James*, ed. Leon Edel and Lyall H. Powers, OUP, 1987, p.195).

Though we cannot be sure what details Henry James knew, Skipsey did resign his curatorship on 31 October 1891 and left Stratford, pleading illness; but Skipsey had indeed, like James's protagonist, lost faith in the supposed 'relics' he was having to introduce and explain. A letter to the editor of the *Times* of 8 September 1903 from J Cuming Walters (editor and author) of Manchester reveals Skipsey's own view that many of the supposed relics of Shakespeare are no such thing, and quotes a letter which Skipsey had written to him soon after his return to Newcastle from Stratford (Skipsey's death had allowed it to be made public), which 'enables me to throw a little light on what has been considered the mystery of his sudden resignation of that position, secured for him by Mr. John Morley'. The date of the letter was 12 May 1893:

> I must not conceal from you the fact that there was another reason (beyond a personal reason specified) why I should resign, and that was that I had gradually lost faith in the so-called relics which it was the duty of the custodian to show, and, if possible, to explain to the visitors at the birthplace. This loss of faith was the result of a long and severe inquiry into which I was driven by questions from time to time put to my wife and me by intelligent visitors; and the effect of it on myself was such as almost to cause a paralysis of the brain . . . That our Shakespeare was born in Henley-street I continue fully to believe (and it was sacred to me on that account); but a man must be in a position to speak in more positive terms than those if he is to fill the post of custodian of that house; and the more I thought of it the more and more I was unable to do this. As to the idle gossip, the so-called traditions and legends of the place, they are for the most part an abomination and must stink in the nostrils of every true lover of our divine poet.

Friends of Skipsey must have noticed that he was unhappy in Stratford, and realised that he would be in need of some money, and so began to look for an increase in his Civil List pension. The *Glasgow Herald* of 29 December 1891 published under the heading of 'Our London Correspondence' the news that

> An earnest effort is, as has already been noted, being made to obtain a Civil List pension for Mr Joseph Skipsey, the North-umberland miner poet. Mr Skipsey has long been known to all interested in the many-sided development of contemporary poetry, and in Northumberland he may fairly be said to be popular. He is best known for his "Carols of the Coal Fields;" but it is a good many years ago now since, by the earlier and less mature work, he gained the high approbation of some of the most competent judges, notably of Dante Gabriel Rossetti and William Morris and Mr Swinburne. His early life was one of hardship. He was an infant when he lost his father, who was shot in an affray between some miners on strike and some special constables, while doing his best to make peace. Young

Skipsey was only seven when he was sent to work in the coal pits, and as his hours of labour extended to sixteen hours a day, it is astonishing how he ever came to find time to teach himself how to read and write. I remember Mr Skipsey telling me some years ago that he learned how to read and write by committing to memory the appearance of the big letters on the placards that used to be stuck up on the hoardings near the pit-mouth. As a trapper-boy in the pit he wrote and ciphered on the "trap-door," in the intervals when no wagon was passing through. He then laboured through grammar, and by slow degrees and some keen native instinct found out and became familiar with the great masterpieces of our literature. He himself began to compose songs and lyrics at an early age, and some of those youthful pieces are among his pleasantest work, with their fresh clear note.

It is now eleven years since the first official notice was taken of Mr Skipsey's claims, as it was in 1880 that a yearly grant of £10 was made to him from the Civil List. In 1886 a special grant of £50 came at an opportune period. Mr Skipsey is now in his sixty-first year, and though a man of noble physique, is now paying nature's penalty of rheumatism for years of privation and exposure, for he was well advanced in life before he left the coal-mines. Lately he obtained the vacant post of custodian of Shakespeare's birthplace at Stratford-upon-Avon, but the change to a southern climate and other reasons of health have compelled him to resign. For all which reasons, as the petition to the Right Hon, Mr Balfour concludes, "some of those who esteem Mr Skipsey as an admirable poet, and as a man of noble and unsullied life, approach Her Majesty's First Lord of the Treasury with the prayer that one who has deserved so well while living, and who will be long remembered when he is dead, may receive such an addition to the small pension he already enjoys as will provide for his declining years." Among the signatures, I may add, are those of certain Northumbrian magnates – e.g., of Lord Percy, Lord Armstrong, Sir Matthew White Ridley, Mr Joseph Cowen, and Dr Spence Watson. Mr John Morley, I believe, has promised his signature, and among those already obtained are the signatures of Professor Edward Dowden, Mr Walter Besant, Mr E Burne Jones, R.A., Mr William Morris, and Mr Theodore Watts.

Meanwhile Mr Skipsey is busy with another edition of his poems – or, rather, with the issue of a restricted and selected collection. The "Songs and Briefer Lyrics" will contain the best of the gallant old Northumberland miner's best pieces (many of them of a grace and beauty of sentiment and purity of expression which is almost Elizabethan), with a few new pieces added. The issue is by subscription, and Mr Skipsey will benefit by the entire proceeds of the sales. There is, I understand, to be a limited edition of 250 numbered copies. The book will be published in January by Mr Walter Scott, of Newcastle.

Christina Rossetti was not as enthusiastic as her brother. In September of 1891 she wrote to Frederic James Shields from Torrington Square:

> I am laying myself out to be disagreeable. Perhaps you guess on what subject. 'The Skipsey Civil List pension.' Do you know pondering the matter I cannot make up my mind that there is *cause shewn* sufficient. Here is a man of vigorous endowments, mental and bodily, able as appears to earn his own livelihood in noble independence but changing from one career because (presumably and I admit it) below his gifts, and from another because of a distasteful superior and perhaps because of long hours. I think 'in this our realm' there must be 'five hundred better than he,' as to genuine claim. So, with your toleration, I recant my promise to sign; and I cheerfully hope that my signing or not signing will not influence the result.

The *Pall Mall Gazette*, ever his supporter, took up the case on 3 May 1892, described the petition and its noteworthy supporters, and added that 'so far it has met with no response' (p. 6).

The *Songs and Lyrics*, mentioned above, collected and revised (London, Walter Scott; limited edition of 250 copies, numbered and initialled) duly appeared. It was reviewed very briefly, though not unflatteringly, in *The Times* of 5 May 1892, but it was rather overshadowed by Kipling's *Barrack-Room Ballads* and W. E. Henley's *Song of the Sword*. 'Mr. Joseph Skipsey, once a working miner himself, and long the poet of the Tyneside miners, must be content to take a lower rank in the hierarchy of contemporary verse than the two writers just noticed. But his more modest muse is not without her special charm, and his SONGS AND LYRICS, collected and revised (London, Walter Scott), will be welcomed by the many who have already discerned in his poetry a vein of genuine, original, and spontaneous inspiration.'

The Era for 28 May 1892, replied to a correspondent called 'The Bard' that 'The curator who did so much to give interest to every object preserved at the Shakespeare House at Stratford-on-Avon, Mr Joseph Skipsey, has resigned the post. He has returned to his native country, and now resides at Newcastle. A volume of his collected poems has just been published.'

Probably more exciting was the invitation to go on a voyage to Norway on a yacht owned by Mr and Mrs J. R. Wood, a young Australian couple. Skipsey had met Fridtjof Nansen, the Norwegian explorer, when he came to Newcastle to give a talk at the Tyne Theatre in February 1892, and he and his hosts visited the yard in which the *Fram* was being built before its launch in 1892. Back in Newcastle, Skipsey became a regular member of Robert Spence Watson's circle; his table talk was said to have been 'trenchant and to the point.' In *Joseph Skipsey: his Life and* Work (T. Fisher Unwin, London, 1909) Watson recalls Skipsey's manner in reciting poetry . . .

> He waited quietly until he felt the spirit of that which he was about to do come upon him. Then he was as one possessed, everything but the poem was forgotten, but that he made live, or perhaps I should more truly say that he incarnated it; he actually became the poem himself. His features changed with every expression of the verse, his hands, nay, even his fingers, expressed the meaning of the words, and that meaning thoroughly revealed itself. It was far beyond what you had thought of, but it stood out clear for you ever afterwards. (p.110)

In his later years Skipsey was very interested in Spiritualism and wrote at length on the topic, believing that he was a 'seer'. James Robertson wrote in his book on *Spiritualism: The Open Door to the Unseen Universe* (London, 1908) that 'Newcastle in the late seventies was . . . the great centre for spiritual work', and reports having met Skipsey, whom he calls 'a notable psychometric medium' (p. 134). Spence Watson was much more sceptical. After going with Skipsey to a séance, Watson seemed to persuade Skipsey that it was not all it claimed to be. He tells us that they ceased to discuss Spiritualism and that he was 'informed by those who were near to him that he abandoned it altogether' (p. 79).

Although the Skipsey's left Stratford in a somewhat dissatisfied frame of mind, he and his wife were fondly remembered. Skipsey's gift for friendship and for maintaining his friends is nowhere better shown than in the letter he wrote to Richard Savage a decade after he left Stratford. It dates from some time between Cuthbert's marriage on July 21 1900 and Joseph's in April 1901:

> 29 Woodbine Street
> Gateshead-on-Tyne
> Many thanks my dear Mr Savage for your welcome letter. In answer to your kind inquiries, I may say that the health of Mrs Skipsey is far from being good, though at present it is a deal better than it has been for a long time. Our sons however are both well & I am glad to say are doing well. Joseph, the eldest, is one of the chief accountants of the Prince Line Shipping Company & Cuthbert is sub-secretary of one of our chief Electric Light Companies – which is a much better position than he held at Scott's Printing Works. He married lately & so is – all right! But Joseph is still with us, & is likely to be for some time to come at least. In fact women don't seem to bother him much & he is too fond of the bicycle, cricket & photography to have any time for sweet hearting. It will interest you to hear that he has developed quite a passion for antiquities & that much of his spare time is devoted to taking photos of the relics of the great Roman Wall. This wall he has been exploring & photographing for some time, with the result that he has now an important collection of photos of it.
>
> You will excuse my writing with the pencil when I tell you I am too much affected with rheumatism to use the pen to any purpose just now, & for the same reason you will kindly excuse the brevity of

my note. Convey our warm regards to Mrs Savage and the family
and
    Believe me very sincerely yours
    Joseph Skipsey

(SBT Collections 93.2)

At the time of the 1901 Census, Joseph Skipsey (69), was living on his means, with his wife Sarah (72) and their son Joseph (31), at 243 Eastbourne Avenue, Gateshead. Sarah Skipsey died on 8 August 1902, aged 73. Joseph died on 3 September 1903, aged 71, at 5 Kells Gardens, Low Fell, Gateshead, the home of his son Cuthbert Skipsey, who was present at his death. On his deathbed, Joseph liked nothing better than to hear the songs of Heine, which Spence Watson's daughter went specially to sing to him (*Joseph Skipsey*, p.21). The death certificate says he died of Cirrhosis of the Liver, which he had been suffering from for four months, according to the doctor, W. R. Sergeant. Joseph and Sarah are buried in Gateshead Cemetery, and on the tombstone are his own lines:

> Oh, what is Life? A magic night
> In which we still to phantoms yield;
> And what is Death, if not the light
> By which the real truth's reveal'd?

They were survived by two sons and a daughter. The obituary in the *Times* reported, with a careless collection of errors, that

> Mr. JOSEPH SKIPSEY, a well-known North Country writer, has died at his residence, Low Fell, near Newcastle-on-Tyne, in his 71st year. Mr. Skipsey, who was known as the "Miner Poet," was born at Percy Main, and during the greater part of his life worked in the mines, going below the surface at the early age of nine years. In 1880, through the influence of Mr. John Morley, M.P., and Dr. Spence Watson he was appointed caretaker of Shakespeare's house, Stratford-on-Avon, but afterwards returned north. Mr. Skipsey, who was self-educated, published five volumes of verse.

Robert Spence Watson published his biography, *Joseph Skipsey, his Life and Work* (London, T. Fisher Unwin) in 1909. In 1912 four poems by Skipsey were included in Sir Arthur Quiller-Couch's *Oxford Book of Victorian Verse*: 'The Violet and the Rose', 'A Merry Bee', 'Dewdrop, Wind and Sun', and 'Mother Wept'. In 1976, Basil Bunting edited *Joseph Skipsey, Selected Poems* (Ceolfrith, Sunderland).

Skipsey maintained throughout his life an honest and direct approach to both life and poetry. As a man, he impressed everyone he met, and as a poet he can do the same. What he wanted from his lyrics can be gathered from what he said in an essay on Longfellow's poems for the *Newcastle Courant* in c.1883. 'They lack the "lilt," which is an indispensable requirement of a good song, and the possession of which enables many a lyric of an apparently humbler character to make the "heart dirl again."' That gladness of the heart is what Skipsey at his best can bring.

Much of the more ephemeral material for this bibliography comes from the two volumes of Skipsey's scrapbooks, bound as *Literary Works* volumes 1 and 2 (L920 S628) held in the Newcastle upon Tyne City Library. The presence of broadsheets of Skipsey's poems (e.g. the 'Epistles to a Brother Rhymer') suggest that Skipsey may well have published other small pamphlets or broadsheets which have not been noticed. The 1858 *Lyrics* and the phantom *The Reign of Gold* (1863?) come into this category.

EDITIONS OF SKIPSEY'S POEMS

1858 *Lyrics*, by J. S., a **Coal Miner.** Durham: George Procter. No copies extant. Reviewed in the *Newcastle Courant* Friday 17 September 1858, (issue 9586. 'Literary Notices').

1859 *Lyrics.* **by Joseph Skipsey.** second edition. Newcastle upon Tyne: Thomas Pigg & Co., Clayton Street. 1859. Printed dedication: 'To Mr. William Reay, Artist, I dedicate the following effusions, as a testimonial of my admiration of those talents which I trust will enable him ere long to take a respectable standing among the artists of our age.' 32pp; 32 poems, printed with fancy red first capitals ornamented with blue. The lithograph portrait preceding a copy in Newcastle City Library is a later addition; it is not in the Robinson Library copy, and, although signed with the initials RH like the 1878 portrait, it is not absolutely identical to it. The Robinson Library copy is inscribed 'Joseph Skipsey to Mr Robt White'. An elegant piece of printing but in paper wrappers only.

1862 *Poems, Songs, and Ballads* (Hamilton & Co., Newcastle upon Tyne). Reviewed anonymously [John Westland Marston] in the *Athenaeum* 1822 (27 September 1862), p. 401.

1863? *The Reign of Gold.* No copy located. Skipsey in publications of this time refers to himself as 'author of 'The Reign of King Gold'. The 1864 *Collier Lad* advertises a reprint of *The Reign of Gold* at two shillings..

1864 *The Collier Lad and other Songs and Ballads* by **Joseph Skipsey,** Author of 'The Reign of Gold,' and other songs and ballads, printed by J. G. Forster, 81 Clayton Street, Newcastle upon Tyne. Twenty-one poems printed with decorative first capitals.

1871 *Poems* by Joseph Skipsey. Blyth. Printed by William Alder. 1871. 59 poems. Decorative first capitals.

1878 *A Book of Miscellaneous Lyrics,* by Joseph Skipsey, author of 'Annie Lee,' 'Two Hazel Eyes.' 'Meg Goldlocks,' 'My Merry Bird,' 'The Fairies Adieu,' and other ditties; Bedlington, printed for the author by George Richardson. With lithographic portrait frontispiece signed with monogram RH, with facsimile in Skipsey's hand: 'Yours truly / Joseph Skipsey'. Printed dedication: 'To Robert Spence Watson, Esq., solicitor, Newcastle-upon-Tyne, as a token of affection and esteem for the man, his culture and his principles, this book is inscribed by his friend the Author. Backworth, August, 1878.' Preface by JS and 48 poems

Reviewed in *The Scotsman*, 25 October 1878.
Reviewed in *The Athenaeum*, 16 November 1878.
Reviewed? In *the Dundee Advertiser*, December 1878.
Reviewed in *The Newcastle Daily Chronicle*, 12 December 1878.
Reviewed? In *The Sunday Times*, 26 January 1879.

1881 *A Book of Lyrics, Songs, Ballads, and Chants,* New edition, revised, London, David Bogue.

1886 *Carols from the Coal-fields; and other Songs and Ballads* (London, Walter Scott), with a biographical note by Robert Spence Watson appended. Sold at 3/6. 'Inscribed to Robert Spence Watson, Esq., LL.D., of Newcastle-upon-Tyne, as a token of sincere regard and affection by the author. Aug. 1886.' 182 poems (counting individually the parts of groups), and Watson's note.

The Robinson library copy is inscribed 'To E. W. Gosse, Esq. with the best regards of the Author Oct. 28 1886' and with a letter tipped in as follows:

186 Dilston Road / Newcastle-on-Tyne / March 12 1892
Dear Mr Gosse,
I hope you will by this time have received from Scott the Publisher a copy of my Songs & Lyrics which I pray you to accept as a token of my continued affection & admiration for you. Hoping that you & dear Mrs Gosse & the rest of your family circle are all well & happy
> I am my dear friend
> Yours Sincerely & Faithfully
> Jospeh Skipsey.

Reviewed in *Newcastle Daily Leader*, October 2 1886
Reviewed in *The Scotsman*, 13 November 1886.

Reviewed in *The Sunday Times,* 21 November 1886.
Reviewed in *Glasgow Herald,* 23 November 1886.
Mentioned in *Saturday Review,* November 1886.
Reviewed in *The Daily News* 17 December 1886.
A notice in the *Newcastle Weekly Chronicle* for 25 December 1887
[?1886] briefly reviewing the book and commenting that it has
been noticed in the *Daily News.*
Reviewed in *The Academy* 22 January 1887, p.53-4 by Walter Lewin.
Review in *Pall Mall Gazette,* 1 February 1887, 'Miner and Minor
Poets' by Oscar Wilde.
Reviewed in *The Mining Journal,* 8 March 1887 by Will Edwardes-
Sprange.
Reviewed in *The Pioneer,* April 1887.
Reviewed in *Newcastle Daily Chronicle,* 5 September 1887.
Reviewed in the *Century Guild Hobby Horse,* 1.6, April 1887.
Reviewed in *The Yorkshire Post*

1888 *Carols, Songs, and Ballads,* by Joseph Skipsey, New edition, London,
Walter Scott, 24 Warwick Lane, Paternoster Row. 1888. [This is a new
edition of *Carols From the Coal Fields.* Skipsey's scrapbook contains a page
of 'Opinions of the Press on *Carols, Songs, and Ballads'* which is made up
of reviews of that book, and includes 'Opinions of the Press on former
Issues, the best of which are comprised in the Carols']. 'Inscribed to
Robert Spence Watson, Esq., LL.D. of Newcastle-upon-Tyne, as a token
of Sincere regard and affection, by the author. Aug, 1886.' The Newcastle
City Library copy of this book has a MS dedication on the half-title: 'To
G. Baker Forster, Esq., / Mining Engineer/ As a token of high Regard & /
deep affection of / his old Servant / The Author / Jan 8, 1889' (George
Baker Forster (1832-1901) was educated at St John's Cambridge – rowing
bow in the Cambridge boat – and became a mining engineer, playing a
significant part in the rescue attempts at the Hartley disaster. He was
interested in education of the miners and got on well with both men and
bosses; he was later Vice-Chairman of the Coal Owners' Association.)
Reviewed in *Newcastle Daily Leader,* 21 November 1888.
Reviewed in *The Comus* [Birmingham] 1 February 1889.
Reviewed in *Birmingham Weekly Mercury,* 2 February 1889.
Reviewed in *Birmingham Daily Post,* 12 June 1889.

1892 *Songs and Lyrics,* collected and revised (London, Walter Scott; limited
edition of 250 copies, numbered and initialled).

Reviewed, by Walter Lewin in *The Academy* XLII, for 20 August 1892, p. 147 'Joseph Skipsey's Songs and Lyrics'.
Reviewed in *Newcastle Daily Leader* 23 May 1892, which mentions a note in the *Pall Mall Gazette*.
Reviewed in *Public Opinion*, 15 April 1892
Reviewed in *The Daily Chronicle*, 23 April 1892.

SKIPSEY AS EDITOR OF THE CANTERBURY POETS

1884   June. 'Canterbury Poets' edition of *Blake* with Introductory Sketch by Joseph Skipsey.

1884   July. 'Canterbury Poets' edition of *Coleridge* with Prefatory Notice by Joseph Skipsey.

1884   August. 'Canterbury Poets' edition of *Shelley* with Prefatory Notice by Joseph Skipsey.

1884   October. 'Canterbury Poets' edition of *Edgar Allan Poe* with Prefatory Notice by Joseph Skipsey.

1885   April. 'Canterbury Poets' edition of *The Poetical Works of Robert Burns*, vol 1, with Prefatory Notice by Joseph Skipsey. Reprinted 1890, 1900.

1885   April. 'Canterbury Poets' edition of *The Poetical Works of Robert Burns*, vol 2, with Prefatory Notice by Joseph Skipsey.

TRANSLATIONS

1863   *Beautés de la poësie anglaise* [title-page says *Rayons et reflects*] by Le Chevalier de Chatelain (London, 1863) translates on pp. 330-331 two poems by Skipsey: 'Un sort heureux' ('A Golden Lot') and 'Chant de depart des fées' ('The Fairies' Parting Song').

The Preface to *Miscellaneous Lyrics* (1878) says that some of the pieces from his 1871 volume were 'honoured by a translation into the French tongue and published in the *Beautés de la Poësie Anglaise par le Chevalier De Chatelain*'. William Reay's *Poems and Lyrics* (1886) says in 'The Author's Preface' that his poems have been translated into French and German.

1863? 'Remarks on Longfellow by Joseph Skipsey author of The Reign of King Gold, &c, &c.' Cutting in Skipsey scrapbook, with the ms annotation 'Printed in the Newcastle Courant about 14 years ago.'

1863 'Shakespeare's Songs' by Joseph Skipsey, Author of "Songs and Ballads," "Discourses on British Lyrists," An essay. *Newcastle Daily Chronicle*, 28 November 1863. Cutting in Skipsey scrapbook.

1876 'Old Ralph, The Furnace Man.' *North of England Review*, August 11, 1876, pp. 54-56. Its first paragraph says 'We were unable last week to complete our extracts from the diary of Mr. Joseph Skipsey, but now have pleasure in doing so.' The extract begins with a letter to Mr. W. H. Robinson of Chester-le-Street, and is dated from Ashington Colliery, near Morpeth on 11 May, 1876. The letter concerns his 'seership', and the editor appends a 'recent specimen of his poetry', "All is Vanity". Cutting in Skipsey scrapbook.

1886 Single sheet printed for private circulation , 'A Rhymed Epistle (On reading some lyrics by an artist and brother poet [William Reay]). By Joseph Skipsey, Author of "Carols from the Coal Fields." 25 stanzas on one side. MS note on the Newcastle City Library copy: 'Kindly return this poem as I am totally out of copies. J.S.'

1886 Single sheet printed for private circulation, 'A Second Epistle to a Brother Rhymer [William Reay]. By Joseph Skipsey, (Author of "Carols from the Coal Fields.")' 28 stanzas on one side.

1887 Printed for private circulation, 'The Rydal Trip, A Rhyme Addressed to a Brother Minstrel. [William Reay] By J. Skipsey. Copy in the scrapbook in the Newcastle City Library.

1888 Skipsey included (introduction and three poems) in *North Country Poets*, ed. William Andrews (London, Manchester and Hull). 1888.

1890 'What is a Poet, and What is Poetry'. An undated cutting in the scrapbook vol 2 writes of a 'series of articles, entitled "The Poet, as Seer and Singer" now appearing in a magazine devoted to literature, art, and philosophy, entitled "Igdrasil". The articles are from the pen of Mr. Joseph Skipsey, the custodian of Shakespeare's Birthplace'. The next three articles seem to be the ones in question.

1890 Printed version of 'The Poet, as Seer, Singer, and Artist. By Joseph Skipsey. Inscribed to R. S. Watson, Esq., LL.D.' Cutting from magazine, in scrapbook, *Literary Works* vol 1 in Newcastle City Library. No indication of where printed. With MS corrections. This and the next two essays are strongly influenced by Spiritualism, and are probably the pieces printed in *Igdrasil*.

1890 'Poetic Inspiration. A Note by Jos. Skipsey. [Being an answer to a question put to the writer on the subject.]' in scrapbook, *Literary Works* vol 1 in Newcastle City Library. No attribution of where printed. Typographically similar to the above. n.d. *Igdrasil*.

1890 'Psychometry. By Joseph Skipsey.' in scrapbook, *Literary Works* vol 1 in Newcastle City Library. No attribution of where printed. Typographically similar to the above. n.d. *Igdrasil*.

1890 Separate printing of *The Poet as Seer and Singer* 'reprinted from "Igdrasil" 1890'.

1891 'The Silent Bird, A Carol' in *Igdrasil*, vol III, September 1891, pp.130-31.

1892 Alfred H. Miles, *The Poets and the Poetry of the Century*, vol V, Charles Kingsley to James Thomson, pp. 515-528; 27 poems in all, with an introduction by Miles.

1898 'The Laureates of Labour. II. – Joseph Skipsey', *The Christian Leader*, 16 March 1898, pp.254-5.

1909 Robert Spence Watson, *Joseph Skipsey, his Life and Work* (London, T. Fisher Unwin)

1924 *Seven Poems by Joseph Skipsey* (The Priory Press, Tynemouth), 21 copies hand printed for private circulation by Robert King

1975 *Joe Skipsey, pitman poet of Percy Main 1832-1903*, edition by the pupils of Preston Grange County Primary School, North Shields.
Reviewed in *Newcastle Journal*, 14 November 1975 by Peter Mortimer.

1976 Basil Bunting, *Joseph Skipsey, Selected Poems* (Ceolfrith, Sunderland).
Reviewed by Garth Clucas in *Agenda*, vol 16, no. 1 (Spring 1978), pp. 106-12.

1878   Theodore   Watts-Dunton,   'Joseph   Skipsey's   Songs   and   Lyrics',
       Athenaeum, 16 November.

1880   'A Miner Poet', in *Capital and Labour: an Economic and Financial Journal*,
       no. 349, Oct 27, price 4d (not seen).

1896   Richard Le Gallienne's review of *Songs and Lyrics*, dated March 1892, is
       reprinted in his *Retrospective Reviews: a Literary Log* (John Lane: The
       Bodley Head) vol.1, pp.73-8.

1909   J. F. Runciman, 'Joseph Skipsey, Poet of the Northumbrian Pits', *Living
       Age*, CCLXII.

1917   *Some Hawarden Letters 1878-1913 written to Mrs. Drew (Miss Mary
       Gladstone) before and after her marriage*, chosen and arranged by Lisle March-
       Phillipps and Bertram Christian (Nesbit & Co, London), pp. 83-6.

1933   B. Ifor Evans, *English Poetry of the Later Nineteenth Century*, chapter xvi.

1974   Martha Vicinus, *The Industrial Muse: Nineteenth-Century British Working-
       Class Literature* (Croom Helm), pp. 141, 143, 155-8, 167, 169-71, 197-8.

1983   Brian Maidment, 'Essayists and Artizans: The Making of Nineteenth-
       Century Self-Taught poets', *Literature and History*, 9, pt. 1 74-91 (p. 79).

1985   H. Gustav Klaus, *The Literature of Labour: 200 Years of Working-Class
       Writing* (Brighton: Harvester) pp. 75-6.

1987   Christopher Ricks (ed), *The New Oxford Book of Victorian Verse* (Oxford
       and New York: Oxford University Press), p. 526.

1987   Brian Maidment (ed), *The Poorhouse Fugitives: Self-Taught Poets and Poetry
       in Victorian Britain* (Manchester: Carcanet) pp. 85-6, 93-4, 186-8, 204-5.

1994   Catherine W. Reilly, *Late Victorian poetry, 1880-1899: an annotated
       biobibliography* (London and New York: Mansell), p. 436.

2000   Catherine W. Reilly, *Mid-Victorian poetry, 1860-1879: an annotated
       biobibliography* (London: Mansell) pp. 421-2.

2000   Vivien Allen (ed), *Dear Mr. Rossetti: The Letters of Dante Gabriel Rossetti
       and Hall Caine 1878-1881* (Sheffield).

2006   S. Bigliazzi, *Collaboration in the Arts from the Middle Ages to the
       Present* (Aldershot: Ashgate).

2005   John Goodridge (ed), *Nineteenth-Century English Labouring-Class Poets*,
       (Pickering and Chatto) vol 3, pp. 211-40.

In volume 2 of Skipsey's scrapbook in Newcastle City Library) is a list of names and addresses, which tells us more eloquently than many pages of biography how wide was Skipsey's circle of friends and how careful he was to keep in touch with his critics..

E Burne-Jones, The Grange, North End Road, West Kensington, London W.
Theodore Watts, The Pines, Putney Hill, London S.W.
A. C. Swinburne, The Pines, Putney Hill, London S.W.
W. M. Rossetti, 5 Endsleigh Gardens, Euston Square, London N.W.
Miss Christina Rossetti, 30 Farrington Square, London W.C.
Richard Garnett LLD, 3 St Edmund's Terrace, Regent's Park S.W.
    Also The British Museum, London.
Austin Dobson, The Board of Trade, Whitehall, London S.W.
Edmund Gosse, The Board of Trade, Whitehall, London S.W.
Andrew Lang, 1 Marloe's Road, Kensington, London W.
Hon. Roden Noel, Annerley Park, London S.E.
W. Tirebuck, The Hill, Coldingham N.B.
Hall-Caine, Aberley, Bexley Heath, By London.
W. Freeland, The Herald Office, Glasgow.
Aubrey De Vere, Curragh Chase, Adare, Ireland.
Walter Lewin, Bebington, Cheshire.
M. Medrington, 44 Milsom Street, Bath.
Miss J. L. Graham, Geo Wilson Esq, Kilmeny – Hawick, N.B.
    Also Hunting Stile, Grasmere, Westmoreland.
W. Edwardes-Sprange, 16 Sansome Street, Worcester.
T. R. Spence, 39 Carden Road, Peckham, London S.E.
    Office 30 Bercer Street, Oxford.
W. Sharp, 46 Talgarth Road, West Kensington, London W.
Miss Emily Pfeiffer, Mayfield, West Hill, Putney, London S.W.
Professor E^d Dowden, Winsted, Temple Road, Rathmines, Ireland.
Miss G Richardson, Hugh Folds, Grasmere, Westmoreland.
A. J. Symington, 10 Battlefield Crescent, Langside, Glasgow.
H. W. Fawcus, 23 Bondgate Without, Alnwick.
Richard Le Gallienne, 85 Oxen Road, Birkenhead.
Herbert P. Horne, 28 Southampton Road, Strand, London W.C.
D. B. W. Sladen, 24A Alfred Place, Thurloe Square, S. Kensington, London.

Rev. Fred Langbridge, St John's Rectory, Limerick, Ireland.

G. J. Robinson, The Shelley Society, 11 Heaton Road, N.C.

Thos Hutchinson, Pegswood, Morpeth.

Sarah Fendley, Messrs Daubarn & Sons, 21 Market Place, Wisbeach, Norfolk.

Charles Sayle, St Mary, Trumpington Rd, Cambridge.

Kineton Parkes, Cavendish Road, Birmingham.

Comins Walters, Editor of the Birmingham Weekly Mercury, Birmingham.

Oscar Wilde, 16 Tite Street, Chelsea, London S.W.

E. Rhys, 13 North Street, Westminster, London.

Mr Crombie, 5 Tenth Avenue, Meldon Terrace.

J Graham Aylward, White Horse Street, Hereford.

T Hudson, Vine Cottage, North Shields.

William Marwick, Edit. of Igdrasil, Hillside House, Arbroath, N. B.

Fredk C. J. Challoner, 3 Grosvenor Gardens, Ealing, W
    (19 Conduit Street, Bond St W) London

Miss Mary Kingan, 20 Mowbray St., Newcastle upon Tyne

Joseph Perrin, 3 Hamsterley Road, Newcastle-upon-Tyne.

Henry C Cor, Market Square, Leighton Buzzard.

Miss M. E. Virebuck, The Hill, Coldingham, Berwickshire.

Geo Lothian, Bee Edge, Coldingham, Berwickshire.

Mrs Cissie Gibson, 4 Percy Terrace, Newcastle-upon-Tyne

Dr H. H. Furness, 222 West Washington Square, Philadelphia, U.S.A.

W. J. Greenstreet, The School House, Cardiff College School.

Mrs James Whitney, 773 Eleventh Street, Oakland, California, U.S.A.

Mrs Gertrude M. Hall, 46 W. Newton Street, Boston, Mass, U.S.A.

E. J. Hanks, Caudu [?] House, 17 Lafayette Place, New York.
    (Or 14 Wall Street)

Mrs Louisa Chandler Moulton, Boston Herald Office, Mass, U.S.A.

Albert Depliley alias A. Buisson-Duberger, 2 Rookley Road, Shepherd's
    Bush Green, London W.

J. Scott Frazer, Liverpool

Earnest Rhys, 2 Heath Cottages, East Heath Road, Hampstead, London

R.G. Hobbs F.R.S., Livingstone House, 374 Wandsworth Road, S.W. London

Fred Shield, Sciena House, Lodges Place, London

Miss A Sharp, Horton House, Rugby

Herbert P. Horne, 20 Fitzroy St, London

Miss Ella Kircum, Leithan, Newnham Road, Bedford.

Mackenzie Bell, Elmstead, Carlton Road, London.

POEMS

A NOTE ON THE POEMS

Whenever Skipsey published a new volume, he took the opportunity to make corrections and alterations to his poems, sometimes changing whole stanzas. We have not always chosen the latest version of the poem to use in the following selection, but we have followed carefully the one which we selected. We have not felt with Basil Bunting that we had the right to 'correct' Skipsey's versions, believing that he took great care with them and meant them as they are.

The 'Epistle to Joseph Skipsey' by William Reay, from his Poems and Lyrics *(West Maitland, 1886), which Skipsey knew, is included because it explains Skipsey's responses and it set him off in a new direction.*

THE SINGER

What tho', in bleak Northumbria's mines,
  His better part of life hath flown,
A planet's shone on him, and shines,
  To Fortune's darlings seldom known:

And while his outer lot is grim,
  His soul, with light and rapture fraught,
Oft will a carol trill, or hymn
  In deeper tones the deeper thought.

A Golden Lot

In the coal-pit, or the factory,
  I toil by night or day,
And still to the music of labour
  I lilt my heart-felt lay;

I lilt my heart-felt lay –
  And the gloom of the deep, deep mine,
Or the din of the factory dieth away,
  And a Golden Lot is mine.

"GET UP!"

"Get up!" the caller calls, "Get up!"
  And in the dead of night,
To win the bairns their bite and sup,
  I rise a weary wight.

My flannel dudden donn'd, thrice o'er
  My birds are kiss'd, and then
I with a whistle shut the door,
  I may not ope again.

Skipsey posing as the pitman poet

The stars are twinkling in the sky,
   As to the pit I go;
I think not of the sheen on high,
   But of the gloom below.

Not rest or peace, but toil and strife,
   Do there the soul enthral;
And turn the precious cup of life
   Into a cup of gall.

O! SLEEP

O sleep, my little baby; thou
    Wilt wake thy father with thy cries;
And he into the pit must go,
    Before the sun begins to rise.

He'll toil for thee the whole day long,
    And when the weary work is o'er,
He'll whistle thee a merry song,
    And drive the bogies from the door.

Lo, a fairy on a day
Came and bore my heart away;
But as she secured her prize,
Sweetest smiles illumed her eyes,
    And, hey, lerry O!

From that moment my career
Lay thro' dells and dingles, where
Pleasure blossom'd out of pain –
Where Joy sang her golden strain,
    Hey, hey, lerry O!

MOTHER WEPT

Mother wept, and father sighed;
  With delight a-glow
Cried the lad, "To-morrow," cried,
  "To the pit I go."

Up and down the place he sped, –
  Greeted old and young;
Far and wide the tidings spread, –
  Clapt his hands and sung.

Came his cronies; some to gaze
  Wrapt in wonder; some
Free with counsel; some with praise;
  Some with envy dumb.

"May he," many a gossip cried,
  "Be from peril kept;"
Father hid his face and sighed,
  Mother turned and wept.

THE BUTTERFLY

The butterfly from flower to flower
   The urchin chased; and, when at last,
He caught it in my lady's bower,
   He cried, "Ha, ha!" and held it fast.

Awhile he laugh'd; but soon he wept,
   When, looking at the prize he'd caught,
He found he had to ruin swept
   The very glory he had sought.

THE DEWDROP

Ah, be not vain. In yon flower-bell,
　　As rare a pearl, did I appear,
As ever grew in ocean shell,
　　To dangle at a Helen's ear.

So was I till a cruel blast
　　Arose and swept me to the ground,
When, in the jewel of the past,
　　Earth but a drop of water found.

THE WIND-BAG

He praised my eyes, so bright and black;
    He praised my locks, so crisp and brown;
My silence sweet – nor was he slack
    My smile to praise – to praise my frown.

From top to toe, me o'er and o'er,
    He praised till – tut! I laugh'd outright;
Against the wind-bag clash'd the door,
    And thro' the key-hole squealed "Good-Night!"

THE DARLING

Misfortune is a darling, ever
Most faithful to the minstrel race;
Let low-bred wretches shun them, never
Yet acted she a part so base.

True, oft by her the bard discovers
He's stript of all he once possest;
But then, just like your sculpture-lovers,
She likes her idols naked, best.

"I hate outlandish things, and own
   I've little liking for the sonnet;
'Tis for a lazy Muse, and one
   Who hath a bumler in her bonnet.

"'Tis a humdrum song, and tho' not long,
   I'd sooner be a kitten, sooner,
And 'Mew!' cry 'Mew!' than listen to
   The ordinary sonnet crooner!"

NOT THE BIRD

He's not the bird I took him for –
   I heard him in the distance screaming,
And tho' his voice was harsh, that hour,
   I dream'd of glories, golden, gleaming!

This hour he meets my closer view;
   And tho' he cuts as big a swagger,
I find a little cockatoo,
   And not a peacock, in the bragger!

My shoulder you pat! What would you be at?
  A bee's in your bonnet I think!
Away, goose, away! if Flit-a-Flirt may,
  Am I to be had at a wink?

There's many a youth the picture of truth,
  As hollow at heart as a pan;
And you – Well, take one, you rook, and begone!
  But another kiss steal, if you can!

TO A STARTLED BIRD
(On Climbing Langrhigg with some friends, 1886.)

Fly not away, wee birdie, pray!
   No weasels we, no evil-bringers,
Would make thee bear the pangs that tear
   Too oft the hearts of sweetest singers.

Long may thy nest with eggs be blest,
   And prove with these brown four, yet fountains
Of tender lays to charm the days
   Of future climbers of the mountains.

"Say, whither goes my buxom maid
 All with the coal-black e'e?"
"Before I answer that," she said,
 "Give ear, and answer me.

"Pray, hast thou e'er thy counsel kept?"
 "Ay, and still can," said he:
"And so can I," said she, and swept
 A-lilting o'er the lea.

LO, THE DAY

Lo the day begins to rise,
    And the shadows of the night,
Overtaken with surprise,
    Blushing fly his presence bright;
Cease thy briny tears to flow,
    Not another murmur sigh;
Thine hath been the cup of woe,
    Now be thine the cup of joy.

Wakened by the voice of morn,
    See, the little urchin Mirth,
How she, laughing Care to scorn,
    Skippeth o'er the jocund earth;
Don, O, don thy best attire,
    Snatch, O, snatch this balm to pain,
Ere the beams of day retire,
    And thy night sets in again.

Annie Lee is fair and sweet –
    Fair and sweet to look upon;
But Annie's heart is all deceit,
    Therefore Annie Lee, begone!

To conceive her smiles, conceive
    Smiles the lily's self might own;
But a snare for me they'd weave:
    Therefore Annie Lee, begone!

Sweeter than a golden bell
    Sound her winning words, each one; –
From a fount of fraud they well;
    Therefore Annie Lee, begone!

In those deep blue orbs, her eyes,
    Pity's built herself a throne;
Pity? Guile in Pity's guise:
    Therefore Annie Lee, begone!

Charming Annie Lee, begone!
    Cunning Annie Lee, begone!
I'd not have thee for a world,
    Tho' so fair to look upon.

LOST AT THE FAIR

Last night at the Fair did I lose thee, my honey –
 I hunted thee south and I hunted thee north;
I'd rather than lost thee have lost all the money
 That all the great lords in the kingdom are worth.

Chorus. – Heart-sorry in worry and flurry did hurry
 Poor I, like a wild thing alost, here and there,
When Rosy the cosy, sweet Rosy the posy
 And pride of her Robin, was miss'd at the Fair.

Resolved to discover the fleet-footed rover,
 My way thro' the stalls, shows, and people I wound;
But there 'mid ways many, the rarest of any,
 No image like Rose's sweet image was found.

Chorus. – Heart-sorry in worry and flurry, etc.

With glee the Inns sounded, with joyance unbounded
 Danced maiden and callant; I into them glanced;
But who was who barely I saw, tho' saw fairly
 That no one like Rose with the dancers a-danced.

Chorus. – Heart-sorry in worry and flurry, etc.

In search of my honey I spent all my money,
 Then took to the road in a spirit of gloom,
When lo, with my Rosy I met, and the posy
 I kiss'd her and cuddled her all the way home.

Chorus. – Heart-sorry in worry and flurry did hurry
 Poor I, like a wild thing alost, here and there;
Till lo, with my Rosy I met, and the posy
 I kiss'd, sung, and linked with her home from the Fair.

THE BRIDAL GIFT

Last night at the Fair I met light-footed Polly
  And Nanny from Earsdon and bothersome Nell;
And yellow-haired Bessy and hazel-eyed Dolly;
  But Rosy for sweetness did bear off the bell.

  Chorus. – Not Polly, nor Dolly, nor coy little Bell;
    Not Nanny, nor Fanny, nor sly little Nell;
    Not Bessy, nor Jessy, is loved half so well
    As Rosy the posy – la, no!

A bridal gift to her – a rich snowy feather,
  To put in her bonnet – a locket I bought;
A hand-bag beside of the best foreign leather;
  A pair of fine gloves and with figures enwrought.

  Chorus. – Not Polly, nor Dolly, etc.

A silken scarf gave I with silver lace laced, and
  A rarely cut comb for her tresses so dear;
A rich broider'd girdle to girdle her waist, and
  A Guinea gold droplet to hang at each ear.

  Chorus. – Not Polly, nor Dolly, etc.

A bonny bit brooch did I buy for her bosom;
  A mantle of scarlet, a bonny white gown;
The garland I'd promised of sweet orange blossom;
  The ring that shall make her forever my own!

  Chorus. – Not Polly nor Dolly, etc.

Some gifts to my honey I bought, and had money
  Been mine, I to these had link'd castles and lands;

And Nan, Nell, and Polly, and Fan, Bell, and Dolly
Had danced in her train and obeyed her commands.

Chorus. – Not Polly, nor Dolly, nor coy little Bell;
Not Nanny, nor Fanny, nor sly little Nell;
Not Bessy, nor Jessy, is loved half so well
As Rosy the posy – la, no!

Plaque from a gift to Joseph Skipsey from the men under his charge.
Image courtesy of Jim Skipsey

THE COLD LOOK

He look'd so cold when last we met;
He never praised my eyes of jet,
But left me here to fret and fret –
He look'd so cold when last we met.

He may not know the pain I dree;
He ever was so kind to me,
I cannot think him cruel, – yet,
He look'd so cold when last we met.

A posy, on his breast did glow;
Who put it there? I'd like to know –
Did neighbour – she? No, no! – and yet,
He look'd so cold when last we met.

I'll to the witch, and if to-night
He frown within her mirror bright,
I'll die, and then, ah, he'll regret
The look he wore when last we met!

My lad he is a Collier Lad,
    And ere the lark awakes,
He's up and away to spend the day
    Where daylight never breaks;
But when at last the day has pass'd,
    Clean washed and cleanly clad,
He courts his Nell who loveth well
    Her handsome Collier Lad.

Chorus – There's not his match in smoky Shields;
    Newcastle never had
A lad more tight, more trim, nor bright
    Than is my Collier Lad.

Tho' doomed to labour under ground,
    A merry lad is be;
And when a holiday comes round,
    He'll spend that day in glee;
He'll tell his tale o'er a pint of ale,
    And crack his joke, and bad
Must be the heart who loveth not
    To hear the Collier Lad.

Chorus – There's not his match, etc.

At bowling matches on the green
    He ever takes the lead,
For none can swing his arm and fling
    With such a pith and speed:
His bowl is seen to skim the green,
    And bound as if right glad

To hear the cry of victory
  Salute the Collier Lad.

  Chorus – There's not his match, etc.

When 'gainst the wall they play the ball,
  He's never known to lag,
But up and down he gars it bound,
  Till all his rivals fag;
When deftly – lo! he strikes a blow
  Which gars them all look sad,
And wonder how it came to pass
  They play'd the Collier Lad.

  Chorus – There's not his match, etc.

The quoits are out, the hobs are fix'd,
  The first round quoit he flings
Enrings the hob; and lo! the next
  The hob again enrings;
And thus he'll play the summer day,
  The theme of those who gad;
And youngsters shrink to bet their brass
  Against the Collier Lad.

  Chorus – There's not his match, etc.

When in the dance he doth advance,
  The rest all sigh to see
How he can spring and kick his heels,
  When they a-wearied be;
Your one-two-three, with either knee
  He'll beat, and then, glee-mad,

114

A heel-o'er-head leap crowns the dance
    Danced by the Collier Lad.

    Chorus – There's not his match, etc.

Besides a will and pith and skill,
    My laddie owns a heart
That never once would suffer him
    To act a cruel part;
That to the poor would ope the door
    To share the last he had;
And many a secret blessing's pour'd
    Upon my Collier Lad.

    Chorus – There's not his match, etc.

He seldom goes to church, I own,
    And when he does, why then,
He with a leer will sit and hear,
    And doubt the holy men;
This very much annoys my heart;
    But soon as we are wed,
To please the priest, I'll do my best
    To tame my Collier Lad.

    Chorus – There's not his match, etc.

THE SEATON TERRACE LASS

My love at Seaton Terrace dwells,
    A hale and hearty wight,
Who lilts away the summer day,
    Also the winter night;
The merriest bird with rapture stirr'd,
    Could never yet surpass
The melody awaken'd by
    The Seaton Terrace lass '

Chorus. – Her like is not in hall or cot;
      And you would vainly pass
      From Tweed to Wear for one to peer
      The Seaton Terrace lass.

She's graceful as a lily-wand,
    Right modest too is she,
And then ye'll search in vain the land
    To find a busier bee;
Like silver clear her iron gear,
    Like burnished gold, the brass –
For tidiness there's none to peer
    The Seaton Terrace lass.

Chorus. – Her like is not, etc.

More restless than a clucking hen
    About her, Minnie stirs;
"Go, jewel, knit your fancy net,
    And I will scour the floors."
"Enjoy the day, a-down the way
    Where greenest grows the grass;
No help I need," replies with speed
    The Seaton Terrace lass.

Chorus. – Her like is not, etc.

116

She'll knit or sew, she'll bake or brew –
  She'll wash the clothes so clean,
The very daisy pales beside
  Her linen on the green;
Then what she'll do, with ease she'll do,
  And still her manner has
A charm would gar a stoic woo
  The Seaton Terrace lass.

Chorus. – Her like is not, etc.

Discomfort flies her dark brown eyes,
  And when the men folk come
All black and weary from the pit,
  They find a welcome home:
Her brothers tease her, and a pride,
  The father feeleth as
Again he meets, again he greets
  The Seaton Terrace lass.

Chorus. – Her like is not, etc.

When day is past and night at last
  Begins to cloud the dell,
She'll take her skiel and out she'll steal,
  And meet me at the well;
Then, oh! how fleet the moments sweet –
  Yet fleeter shall they pass,
That night the Bebside laddie weds
  The Seaton Terrace lass.

Chorus. – Her like is not in hail or cot,
    And vainly would you pass
  From Tweed to Wear for one to peer
    The Seaton Terrace lass.

As I came down from Earsdon Town,
  Upon an Easter day,
Whom did I meet but she, the sweet,
  The blue-eyed Lotty Hay.

A crimson blush her cheek did flush,
  Nor sin did that betray;
The pearl is sure a jewel pure,
  And so is Lotty Hay.

All evil flees her heart, yet she's
  To Slander's shafts a prey,
And words of ill do nearly kill
  The lowly Lotty Hay.

Some deem her proud; in speech aloud
  Some other yet will say
She's cold or fierce, and all to pierce
  The heart of Lotty Hay.

Proud? – She's not proud: to-day I view'd
  An ant beside her stray,
And that wee thing kind blinks did bring
  From soft-eyed Lotty Hay.

Fierce? – She's not fierce; a fly did pierce –
  Late pierce her bosom, yea,
And made her cry, yet that bad fly
  Was spared by Lotty Hay.

Not proud nor bold, not fierce nor cold,
  But meek, kind, mild alway –

A soul of light did meet my sight
    As I pass'd Lotty Hay.

Upon her way she went and, nay,
    Not lighter moved to-day
The thistle-down then upward flown,
    Than walked this Lotty Hay.

In cotton gown she tript to town,
    And not a lady gay
In satin drest could be more blest
    Than seemed sweet Lotty Hay.

TWO HAZEL EYES

Was ever a bard in such pitiful plight?
   Was ever such seen by yon stars in the skies?
A-pit or a-bed – by day and by night,
   I'm plagued by the magic of two hazel eyes.

A leaf in a whirlwind, I'm sent to and fro,
   And peace, panic-stricken, my bosom still flies;
For rest I implore, but my portion below
Is the rest-killing magic of two hazel eyes.

The world it goes up, and the world it goes down,
   And the lofty descend, and the lowly arise;
But fortune, the filter, may smile or may frown,
   I feel but the magic of two hazel eyes.

Once blithe as a linnet I lilted my lay,
   And won the applause of both foolish and wise –
Now deaf, dumb, derided, I go on my way,
   Bewitched by the magic of two hazel eyes.

O Annie, wouldst thou but look down on my plight,
   And pity my case, and no longer despise,
I'd dance in delight, I'd sing day and night,
   And the theme of my lays be thy two hazel eyes!

MEG GOLDLOCKS

Ye've heard of Meg Goldlocks of Willington Dene?
The stoniest damsel that ever was seen;
Yet, her beauty distress'd, with its splendour, the rest
Of the lasses for miles around Willington Dene.

Meek Mary of Howdon, with Robin would rove!
But once to the Dene did his merry feet move,
A-jealous of Meg's unmatched beauty, her tongue
Was turned to a bell, and a golden peal rung!

Blithe Betsy of Percy, eyed Jim like a spy,
Lest o'er to the Dene he should slip on the sly;
Nay, did she but dream it, with heart like to break.
She scowled when she met him for all the next week.

Sweet Nancy of Benton, deemed Willie her own,
Till he went to the Dene on an errand unknown
The errand to her was apparent as day,
And the rose on her dimpled cheek withered away.

Thus matters went on around Willington Dene,
Till East came a gallant and married the quean;
That moment the rest of the lasses were blest,
And their lovers allowed to tread Willington Dene!

THE LAD OF BEBSIDE

My heart is away with the lad of Bebside,
And never can I to another be tied;
Not, not to be titled a lord's wedded bride,
Could Jinny abandon the lad of Bebside.

He dances so clever, he whistles so fine,
He's flattered and wooed from the Blyth to the Tyne,
Yet spite of the proffers he meets far and wide,
I'm alone the beloved of the lad of Bebside.

He entered our door on the eve of the Fair,
And cracked with our folk in a manner so rare,
Next morning right early with spleen I was eyed
To link to the Fair with the lad of Bebside.

Last night at the dancing, 'mid scores of fine queans,
The eldest among them just out of her teens,
He chose me, and truly with pleasure and pride
I footed the jig with the lad of Bebside.

To wed me he's promised, and who can believe
A laddie like him can a lassie deceive?
The moon's on the wane – ere another be spied,
I'll lie in the arms of the lad of Bebside.

YOUNG FANNY

A change hath come over young Fanny,
  The yellow-hair'd lass of the Dene –
Erewhile she look'd cosy and canny,
  But now – now, what aileth the queen?

Erewhile she'd the bearing which blesses
  The heart of the weary and worn,
Now all Percy Main she distresses,
  And burdens the air with her scorn.

Erewhile she was sweet as the lily,
  And mild as the lamb on the lea;
Now sour as the docken, and truly
  More fierce than a tiger is she.

Erewhile she would play with the kitten,
  Averse to contention and strife;
Now Tab on the house-top is sitting,
  And dare not come down for her life.

"What aileth the jewel?" Quoth granny;
  "What aileth the winds when they blow?
When the reason's no secret to Fanny,
  The reason we mortals may know."

ANNIE

Coal black are the tresses of Fanny;
    But never a mortal could see
The coal-coloured tresses of Annie,
    And be as a body should be.

White, white, is her forehead, and bonnie –
    And when she goes down to the well,
The beat of the footstep of Annie,
    The wrath of a tiger would quell.

Red, red, are her round cheeks and bonnie –
    And when she is knitting, her tone –
The charm of the accents of Annie,
    Would ravish the heart of a stone.

Nay, rare are her graces and many,
    But nothing whatever can be
Compared to the sweet glance of Annie, –
    The glance she has given to me.

MARY OF CROFTON

Ah! a lovely jewel was Mary of Crofton,
    And now she is cold in the clay,
We think of the heart-cheering image as often
    As we pass down the old waggon way.

Her air was a magical air, and the very
    Stone heart of the stoic entranced;
While her wee, wee feet beat a measure as merry
    As ever by damsel was danced.

Her accent enchanted; her lay -- but the silly
    Bit linnet to vie it would seek;
And the rose in her hair was a daffodowndilly
    Compared with the rose on her check.

Sue, Bessy, and Kitty still ornament Crofton,
    And rich are the charms they display;
But we miss the sweet image of Mary as often
    As we pass down the old waggon way.

HEY ROBIN
(*The first two lines are old*)

Hey Robin, jolly Robin,
    Tell me how thy lady doth?
Is she laughing, is she sobbing,
    Is she gay, or grave, or both?

Is she like the lark, so merry,
    Lilting in her father's hall?
Or the crow with cry a very
    Plague to each, a plague to all.

Is she like the violet breathing
    Blessings on her native place?
Or the cruel nettle scathing
    All who dare approach her grace?

Is she like the dew-drop sparkling
    When the morn peeps o'er the land?
Or the cloud in mid-air darkling,
    When a fearful storm's at hand?

Tut, to count the freaks of woman,
    Count the pebbles of the seas;
Rob, thy lady's not uncommon,
    Be or do she what she please!

THE GOLDEN BIRD

I will not hear one cruel word,
Or how he sinn'd, or how he err'd;
He's yet to me the golden bird
    He ever was to Dora!

I met him on the street to-day,
In haste to meet my rival gay;
He turn'd from me his face away!
    – Yet, yet he's dear to Dora.

Into a floral shop he went,
I knew too well with what intent;
Ah, not for me the wreath was meant!
    – Yet, yet he's dear to Dora.

While I sit here a weary wight,
He with my foe, to her delight,
Will dance his bridal dance to-night!
    – Yet, yet he's dear to Dora.

My heart is rent: he's sore to blame;
Yet blame him not, or kindly blame;
I cannot hear a word would shame
    The golden bird of Dora!

SLIGHTED

Ah me! my heart is like to break,
The envied rose upon my cheek,
The blood red rose is cold and bleak
    Now Robin slighteth me.

Alas! a shadow lone and pale,
I all unheard my lot bewail;
He listens to another's tale,
    He hath no ear for me.

Could he but look upon my grief,
Would he not try to bring relief?
I feel my days below are brief,
    So deep the wound I dree.

I trail about I know not how,
I like a thief slink down the row,
For well behind my back I know,
    The rest all laugh at me.

The rest to one the other wink
Whenever down the row I slink;
Their hearts are filled with glee to think
    How he my bane should be.

The very bairns have caught their words,
As notes are caught by mocking birds;
By jibes are rent my bosom chords,
    And grief is killing me.

I feel my days on earth are brief;
Ah! could he look upon my grief,

Would he not try to bring relief?
  Would he not kinder be?

I dreamed last night to me he came;
A blush was on his cheek for shame;
He took my hand, he breathed my name,
  He gave such looks to me –

Such looks? No sun will rise or set
When I forget those looks, forget
Those star-bright eyes, those eyes of jet,
  That wiled my heart from me.

The vision fled, and I was left
To mourn a lot of hope bereft –
To mourn what won my heart, and cleft,
  And oh, the agony!

Dear Robin – Dear? Without a peer,
And yet to me so dear, so dear!
Ah, fare-thee-well! and may'st thou ne'er
  Be doomed to sigh like me!

THE OUTCAST FLOWER

You turn up your nose at me? I suppose
  I'm noisome and base?
Before on my head you cruelly tread,
  Give ear to my case.

A lily-bell rare, my charms were laid bare,
  And lo! at the sight,
In a mantle of gold, a delight to behold,
  Love danced in delight.

To him I was dear – ah me! it was clear
  That nothing above,
Below, or around, on earth could be found,
  So precious to love.

That little white flower which gildeth the hour
  When March winds rave,
The snowdrop, as clear from stain might appear,
  But look'd too grave.

The crocus a-drest in her sun-given vest,
  On Spring's live mould,
To her heart's delight, might sparkle as bright,
  But look'd too bold.

No zephyr did woo a hyacinth blue,
  With bearing so fine;
No daffodil e'er did view in the mere
  A face so divine.

The tulip so gay a cheek might display
  In deeper hues dyed;

But where the sweet smell? – could any one tell? –
    The dancer enjoyed?

The pink had a bloom as rich in perfume,
    To make the heart glad;
But where was the grace to rivet the gaze
    The lily-bell had?

Not even the rose, the richest that blows,
    Could Love then prefer;
And the pansy, so sweet, bowed down at her feet,
    In homage to her.

This swore Love, and, sworn, away I was torn,
    His pleasure to be;
But ere a day past away I was cast –
    He cared not for me.

Unheeded I pined, my sweets did the wind
    No longer perfume;
To vile turned the pure – the sweet turned a sour –
    Ah, such was my doom.

You turn up your nose! just think of my woes,
    Though base to behold,
Just think ere you tread – ere you crush my poor head –
    Just think what I've told.

Eleven long winters departed
 Since you and he sailed o'er the main?
Dear, dear – I've been thrice broken-hearted,
 And thrice – but, ah, let me refrain. –

There was not a lassie in Plessy,
 Nay, truly there was not a lad,
That morning you left us all, Bessy,
 But dropped a kind tear and look'd sad.

A week ere ye went ye were married –
 Yes, yes, I remember aright;
The lads and the lassies all hurried
 To dance at your bridals that night.

With others, were Mary from Horton,
 And Harry from over the fields;
Your prim cousin Peggy from Chirton,
 And diddler Allen from Shields.

Piper Tom, with his pipes in the corner,
 Did pipe till the red morn a-broke;
And we danced and we sung in our turn, or
 Gave vent to our glee in a joke.

That seems but last night, tho' eleven
 Black winters have flown since, and yet
Ye're bright as yon star in the heaven,
 Whilst I – but I winnot regret.

Ye're just bright and fresh and as rosy,
 As when ye last left us all, just;

Whilst I am a poor wither'd posy
  The passer has strampt in the dust.

This was not so always; no, clearly
  – When lassies – the burnie has shown
The rose on your dimpled cheek nearly
  Out-matched by the rose on my own.

Twinn'd sisters appeared we, and canny
  Together we'd link o'er the wold,
When Bessy's bit secrets to Nanny,
  And Nanny's to Bessy were told.

Nay's one, we grew up until Harry
  Was mine – but, was mine for how long?
Then, the changes that followed, – the worry,
  The guilt, and the shame, and the wrong?

– Ye knew my 'curst bane and besetter?
  Brown? Piers with the thievish black e'e?
He danced at your wedding, and better
  Than any but Harry danced he.

The sight sent the lasses a-skarling,
  Whenever he came into view;
And many a fond mother's darling
  Has lived his deception to rue.

Meg Wilson, a-down the green loaning,
  Skipped with him a fine afternoon;
When last she went there she was moaning,
  Her heart like a harp out of tune.

Even Cary, the dour-looking donnet,
      Who'd looked on my downfall with scorn,
Was smit with his blink, and her bonnet
      One Monday was found in the corn.

Nay, many with him tripped and tumbled
      As I'd tripped and tumbled – what then?
Not one by her fall was so humbled,
      Or put to one half of my pain.

When Harry was brought on a barrow,
      A corpse from the pit, had I known
– But Brown, who had long been his marrow,
      Then, who was so kind as Piers Brown?

He showed himself ready and willing
      To lighten the load I endured;
He gather'd me many a shilling,
      And whatso I needed procured.

The bones of my Harry right duly
      Were laid in the grave by his aid;
Then slipt he to see me – too truly
      So slipt till my pride was low laid.

There's many to point and to titter
      At one who has happen'd a fall
And into the cup that is bitter,
      The petty still empty their gall.

Then, mine was a hardship and trouble;
      When touch'd by deceit's magic mace,
My pride went away like a bubble,
      Mine, mine was a pitiful case.

134

Then deep on my cheek burn'd the scarlet,
    The token of sin and of shame;
And many did call me a harlot,
    More worthy than I of the name.

Then mishap to mishap, like billow
    To billow succeeded, and I
Was laid with my head on my pillow,
    And no one to comfort me nigh.

Then perished the darlings you kindly
    Remember to ask for – alone
I lay by the morsels and blindly
    Then cursed the dark hour I was born.

A-lorn by the dead lay I – driven
    To frenzy by grief, shame, and scorn,
And lifted my two hands to heaven,
    Then cursed the dark hour I was born.

I cursed – felt accursed – nay, that hourly
    I'd dogg'd by a black devil been;
And he, when he'd speeded more surely,
    Had held in derision my teen.

He'd dazzled and led me to yamour,
    For baubles one ought to despise,
Then whipt from my vision the glamour,
    And shown the sad truth to my eyes.

He'd mounted the air, and a snelling
    Bleak blast had swept valley and plain;
And the dwelling of joy made the dwelling
    Of dire desolation and pain.

Years long the keen thought of the cruel
   Black lot of thy crony a-led
Her to feel, and to prate thus, and – jewel! –
   Yet puts a mill-wheel in her head.

The pale morning finds me a-wringing
   My hands for the dearies in vain;
The day passes by without bringing
   Me any relief to my pain.

Evermore on my heart feeds the canker,
   The cruel reflection that – ay –
That they for a morsel did hanker,
   I had not a penny to buy.

Overcome by despair in confusion
   Of mind, I will wander oft, when
The prey of a charming delusion.
   They seem to be living again.

Again on their hazels a-prancing,
   They hie as they hied o'er the way;
The midges above them a-dancing,
   Are not half so merry as they.

Again up and down the ball boundeth
   A-tween their bit hands and the earth,
Till rapture their senses confoundeth,
   And laughter gives vent to their mirth.

Again – in my sight – my woe banished, –
   The birds seem a-living again,
Then quickly I find them a-vanished,
   And sorrow yet with me, and pain.

While yet but a lassie, I married;
　　While yet in my teens I was left;
Ere olden to frenzy was harried –
　　Ere olden of hope I'm a-reft.

A reed by the wild wind a-broken
　　Am I, and my tongue in vain seeks
To utter the tale which a-spoken,
　　Would hurry that rose from your cheeks.

But let me refrain. Since we parted –
　　Ah lass, since ye went o'er the main;
Since then I've been thrice broken-hearted –
　　And thrice – but ah, let me refrain.

CRUEL ANNA

Little Anna, cruel elf,
  Spite of all my reason,
She yet puts me from myself
  In and out of season;
Ah, the may, ah, the fay,
  Glee to mischief wedded!
Foe to rest, she's a pest,
  And always to be dreaded!

  Chorus. – Ah, the may, ah, the fay, –
      Glee to mischief wedded!
      Foe to rest, she's a pest –
      And always to be dreaded!

Never goes the sun around,
  But upon me stealing,
She, she doth my soul confound,
  Sends my reason reeling;
Gars me sing, and while, alack,
  I in glee am singing,
On me turns and in a crack,
  Gives my ear a-wringing.

  Chorus. – Ah, the may, etc.

Pat she comes and goes, the wasp!
  Back anon she hummeth;
Round my neck her hands to clasp,
  That to do she cometh;
So she leads me to suppose
  By her air entrancing,

Till I'm twitted by the nose
   And again sent dancing.

   Chorus. – Ah, the may, etc.

Ear or nose, or wrung or stung,
   'Tween a thumb and finger,
How to be avenged now long
   Lost in doubt I linger;
Then when I resolved at last
   Rush her pride to humble;
Lo, o'er me a glamour cast,
   O'er the stools I tumble.

   Chorus. – Ah, the may, etc.

Head a-turned, heart a-burned,
   Nay, reduced to cinders;
Nose a-stung, ears a-wrung,
   Shins all sent to flinders;
Pale and thin, bone and skin –
   I'm a spectre merely;
And he who'd play my part might say
   He'd bought his whistle dearly.

   Chorus. – Ah, the may, etc.

HAUNTED

Little Anna young and fair,
   How with heart a-dancing,
I descry her image rare,
   O'er the footway glancing;
Ah, those locks of dusky hue,
   Ah, those eyes that twinkle,
Now I laugh their sheen to view,
   Now my tears down trinkle!

Rare her grace, her bearing rare,
   Meteor-like she glideth;
And where'er she glideth, there
   Some dire ill betideth.
In the earth or in the air
   Lo, an imp abideth
All, to whelm in despair
   He who love derideth.

So do I – I who love mocked –
   Feel unto my anguish,
In love's magic fetters locked
   Night and day I languish;
Not a bit of use am I,
   Save with arms a-kimbo,
Thus to sit and thus to sigh,
   And wish myself at limbo.

Oft from tossings to and fro,
   Bite or sup unheeded
Up, from bed to work I'll go
   Long before it's needed.

But a-pit, love a-smit,
    Do all I can do now;
Still a-wry the pick will fly,
    And no coal will hew, now.

Can it be her voice I hear,
    When my pick is swinging?
When her tongue attracts the ear,
    Golden bells are ringing:
Do I dream? or is't her e'en
    Yonder nook adorning?
Blacker than the coal, their sheen
    Mocks the coal a-burning.

Daily – hourly, by the elf
    I, who love derided,
Witched – nay lost am to myself, –
    From myself divided:
Lost? – I'm cross'd and tempest toss'd
    On a sea of passion,
And shall so remain while, lo!
    There's a rock to dash on!

Ah, those locks, and ah those eyes!
    Ah, the rest they've broken!
But in vain their victim tries –
    Love can ne'er be spoken:
Man may fathom ocean – say
    The reason of its motion,
But Love's magic never – nay,
    It's deeper than the ocean.

The Hartley men are noble, and
    Ye'll hear a tale of woe;
I'll tell the doom of the Hartley men –
    The year of Sixty-two.

'Twas on a Thursday morning, on
    The first month of the year,
When there befell the thing that well
    May rend the heart to hear.

Ere chanticleer with music rare
    Awakes the old homestead,
The Hartley men are up and off
    To earn their daily bread.

On, on they toil; with heat they broil,
    And streams of sweat still glue
The stour unto their skins, till they
    Are black as the coal they hew.

Now to and fro the putters go,
    The waggons to and fro,
And clang on clang of wheel and hoof
    Ring in the mine below.

The din and strife of human life
    Awake in "wall" and "board,"
When, lo! a shock is felt which makes
    Each human heart-beat heard.

Each bosom thuds, as each his duds
    He snatches and away,

142

And to the distant shaft he flees
　With all the speed he may.

Each, all, they flee – by two – by three
　They seek the shaft, to seek
An answer in each other's face,
　To what they may not speak.

"Are we entombed?" they seem to ask,
　"For the shaft is closed, and no
Escape have we to God's bright day
　From out the night below."

So stand in pain the Hartley men,
　And swiftly o'er them comes
The memory of home, nay, all
　That links us to our homes.

Despair at length renews their strength,
　And they the shaft must clear;
And soon the sound of mall and pick
　Half drowns the voice of fear.

And hark! to the blow of the mall below
　Do sounds above reply?
Hurra, hurra, for the Hartley men,
　For now their rescue's nigh.

Their rescue nigh? The sounds of joy
　And hope have ceased, and ere
A breath is drawn a rumble's heard
　Re-drives them to despair.

Together, now behold them bow;
  Their burden'd souls unload
In cries that never rise in vain
  Unto the living God.

Whilst yet they kneel, again they feel
  Their strength renew'd – again
The swing and the ring of the mall attest
  The might of the Hartley men.

And hark! to the blow of the mall below
  Do sounds above reply?
Hurra, hurra, for the Hartley men
  For now their rescue's nigh.

But lo! yon light, erewhile so bright
  No longer lights the scene;
A cloud of mist yon light hath kiss'd,
  And shorn it of its sheen.

A cloud of mist yon light hath kiss'd,
  And see! along must crawl,
Till one by one the lights are smote,
  And darkness covers all.

"O, father, till the shaft is cleared,
  Close, close beside me keep;
My eye-lids are together glued,
  And I – and I – must sleep."

"Sleep, darling, sleep, and I will keep
  Close by – heigh-ho!" – To keep
Himself awake the father strives –
  But he – he too – must sleep.

"O, brother, till the shaft is cleared,
    Close, close beside me keep;
My eye-lids are together glued,
    And I – and I – must sleep."

"Sleep, brother, sleep, and I will keep
    Close by – heigh-ho!" – To keep
Himself awake the brother strives;
    But he – he too – must sleep.

"O, mother dear! wert, wert thou near
    Whilst sleep!" – The orphan slept;
And all night long by the black pit-heap
    The mother a dumb watch kept.

And fathers and mothers, and sisters and brothers –
    The lover and the new-made bride –
A vigil kept for those who slept,
    From eve to morning tide.

But they slept – still sleep – in silence dread,
    Two hundred old and young,
To awake when heaven and earth have sped,
    And the last dread trumpet rung!

BEREAVED

One day as I came down by Jarrow,
  Engirt by a crowd on a stone,
A woman sat moaning and sorrow
  Seized all who gave heed to her moan.

"Nay, blame not my sad lamentation,
  But oh, let" she said, "my tears flow,
Nay offer me no consolation —
  I know they are dead down below."

I heard the dread blast and I darted
  Away on the road to the pit,
Nor stopped till my senses departed,
  And left me the wretch I here sit.

"Ah, thus let me sit," so entreated
  She those who had had her away;
Then yet on the hard granite seated,
  Resumed her lament and did say: —

"My mother, poor body, would harry
  Me still with a look sad and pale,
When I had determined to marry
  The dimpled-chinn'd lad of the dale.

"Not that she had any objection
  To one praised by each and by all;
But ay his lot caused a reflection
  That still, still her bosom would gall.

"Nay, blame not my sad lamentation;
  My mother sleeps under the yew —

She views not the dire desolation
　　She dreaded one day I should view.

"Bedabbled with blood are my tresses?
　　No matter! Unlock not my hand! —
When first I enjoyed his caresses,
　　Their hue would his praises command.

"He'll never praise more locks nor features,
　　Nor, when the long day-tide is o'er,
With me view our two happy creatures;
　　With bat and with ball at the door.

"Nay, chide not. A pair either bolder
　　Or better nobody could see:
They passed for a year or two older
　　Than what I could prove them to be.

"Their equals for courage and action
　　Were not to be found in the place;
And others might boast of attraction,
　　But none had their colour or grace.

"Their feelings were such, tho' when smitten
　　By scorn, still their blood would rebel;
They wept for the little blind kitten
　　Our neighbour did drown in the well.

"The same peaceful, calm, and brave bearing,
　　Had still been the father's was theirs;
And now we felt older a-wearing,
　　We deemed they'd soon lighten our cares.

147

"So doomed I last night. On his shoulder
    I hung and beheld them at play:
I dreamed not how soon they must moulder
    Down, down in their cold bed of clay.

"Chide, chide not. This sad lamentation
    But endeth the burden began,
When to the whole dale's consternation,
    Our second was crushed by the van.

"That dark day the words of my mother
    In all the deep tone which had made
Me like a wind-ridden leaf dother,
    Rang like the dead bell in my head.

"Despair, the grim bird away chidden,
    Would light on the house-top again;
But still from my husband was hidden
    Each thought that had put him to pain.

"He's pass'd from existence unharried
    By any forbodings of mine;
Nor till we the lisper had buried,
    E'er pined he. But then he did pine.

"Down when the dark shadow had falling
    Across the long row gable-end,
He miss'd him when home from his calling,
    With thrice weary bones he would wend.

"No more would his heavy step lighten,
    No more would his hazel eyes glow;
No more would his smutty face brighten
    At sight of the darling. Ah, no!

"He lived by my bodings unharried,
    But when from his vision and mine,
Away the sweet lisper was carried
    He pined, and long after would pine.

"Ay, truly.—And reason.—The sonsy—
    The bairn with his hair bright and curled,
He still had appeared to our fancy,
    The bonniest bairn in the world.

"As ruddy was he as a cherry,
    With dimple on chin and on cheek;
And never another as merry
    Was seen to play hide-and-go-seek.

"Yet, yet with his fun and affection,
    His canny bit pranks and his grace,
He wheedled my heart from dejection,
    And put a bright look on my face.

"Full oft upon one leg advancing,
    Across to the door he would go;
Wheel round on his heel, then go dancing
    With hop after hop down the row.

"When—Let my hand go!—When he perish'd,
    The rest were a balm to my woe:
But now, what remains to be cherish'd?
    But now, what remains to me now?

"Barely cold was the pet ere affected
    By fever they lay one and all;
But lay not like others neglected;
    I slept not to be at their call.

"Day and night, night and day without slumber,
    I watched till so weary and worn;
When Death took the gem of the number,
    I'd barely strength left me to mourn.

"I've mourn'd enough since. And tho' cruel
    Mishap like a curs'd hag would find
Her way to my door still, the jewel
    Has seldom been out of my mind.

"Another so light and so airy
    Ne'er gladden'd a fond mother's sight—
I oft heard her called a wee fairy,
    And heard her so called with delight.

"Whilst others played, by me she tarried,
    —The cherub!—and rumour avers
That now-a-days many are married,
    With not half the sense that was hers.

"A-down on the hearth-rug a-sitting
    The long winter nights she was heard,
The while her sweet fingers were knitting,
    To lilt out her lay like a bird.

"Did I appear cross? To me stealing,
    Askance in my face she would keek;
At which, e'er the victim of feeling,
    I could not but pat her bit check.

"Once, when I had pricked this hard finger—
    No, he who in grave-clothes first slept;
No, she—with the senses that linger
    I cannot tell which of them—wept.

"She vanished at last. Ah, an ocean
    Of trouble appeared that black cup,
But what was it all to the potion
    I now am commanded to sup.

"My husband, my birdies, my blossoms!
    Well—well—I am wicked—yes, yes;
But take my case home to your bosoms,
    And say if your sin would be less?

"The dear ones to perish thus sudden
    Not only last night by the hearth—
This morn when resuming their dudden,
    E'en they, the dear bairns, were all mirth.

"Aroused by their voices—a-yearning
    To kiss them I sprang to the floor,
They kissed me and bade me good morning,
    And whistled away from the door.

"Long after away they had hurried,
    Their music a-rang in my ears;
Then thought I of those we had buried,
    And thought of the jewels with tears.

"Then thought I—what said I—thus thinking
    Was I, when rat-tat went the pane,
And back into sense again shrinking,
    I thought of the living again.

"Anon gaining nerve I endeavour'd
    To open the door, when some-how
The sneck from my fingers was severed,
    And back into bed I did go.

"Did I sleep? I did sleep. To his calling
    The father had gone hours before,
And now in that havock appalling,
    He lies with the blossoms I bore.

"Did I sleep? I did sleep. Heart-a-weary,
    How oft have I so wept before;
Not to weep but to sleep, lone and dreary
    I've wandered the broken brick floor.

"Did I sleep?—well, your kind arm and steady
    My tottering steps, and now you
Go, get out the winding sheets ready,
    And do what remaineth to do.

"Spread winding sheets—one for the father,
    And two for the darlings, our pride,—
And one for the wife and the mother,
    All, soundly she'll sleep by their side!"

'Twas on a night, with sleet and snow
 From out the north a tempest blew,
When Thistle gathered nerve to go
 The little Nettle's self to woo.

Within her father's cottage soon
 He found the ever-dreaded maid;
She then was knitting to a tune
 The wind upon the window played.

His errand known, she, with a frown,
 Up from the oaken table sprung,
Down took the broom and swept the room,
 While like a bell her clapper rung.

"Have I not seen enough to be
 Convinced for ever, soon or late,
The maid shall rue the moment she
 Attendeth to a wooer's prate?

"How long ago since Phemie Hay
 To Harry at the Mill fell wrong?
How long since Hall a prank did play
 On silly Nelly Brown? – how long?

"How long ago since Adam Smith
 Wooed Annie on the Moor, and left
The lassie with a stain? yea, with
 A heart of every hope bereft?

"But what need instance cases? lo!
 Have I not heard thee chaunt the lay,

153

'The fraud of men was ever so
　　Since summer first was leafy?' eh?

When men are to be trusted, then,
　　– But never may that time befall;
Of five times five-and-twenty men,
　　There's barely five are men at all.

"Before the timid maid they'll fall,
　　And smile and weep and sigh and sue,
Till once they get her in their thrall,
　　And then she's doomed her lot to rue.

"For her a subtle snare they weave,
　　And when the bonny bird is caught,
Then, then they giggle in their sleeve;
　　Then laugh to scorn the ill they've wrought.

"As other weary winds, they woo
　　The bloom its treasures to unfold;
Extract its wealth – their way pursue,
　　And leave her pining on the wold.

"When poppies fell like lilies smell,
　　When cherries grow on brambles, when –
When grapes adorn the common thorn,
　　Then women may have faith in men.

"Then may we hear what they may swear;
　　Till then, sir, know I'm on my guard,
And he, the loon that brings me down,
　　He, he'll be pardoned, on my word."

Thus for an hour her tongue was heard;
   By this, her words grown faint and few,
She raised the broom at every word,
   And thumped the floor to prove it true.

In ardent words the youth replied:
   "Dread hollow-hearted guile thou must;
But deem not all of honour void,
   Nor punish all with thy mistrust.

"A few, not all, the lash have earn'd,
   Let but that few the lash assail;
The world were topsy-turvy turned,
   Did not some sense of right prevail.

"Destroy the weed, but spare the flower;
   Consume the chaff, but keep the grain;
Nor harry one who'd die before
   He'd give thy little finger pain."

On hearing this, she sat her down,
   Took up her needlework again,
And tho' she strove to wear a frown
   Made answer in a milder strain.

"Forego thy quest. Deceitful words
   May yet, as they have been, may be
A fatal lure to lighter birds;
   They'll never prove the like to me.

"Still by my chastity I vow,
   As I have kept the cheat at bay,
So, should I keep my senses, so
   I'll keep him till my dying day.

"The best that man can do or say,
  The love of gold or rubies rare, –
Not all that wealth can furnish, may
  Once lure to leave me in a snare.

"So end thy quest." He only prest
  His ardent suit the more, while she
At every word he uttered, garr'd
  Her fleeing needles faster flee.

"My quest by honour's justified;
  I long have eyed and found thee still
The maid I'd like to be my bride;
  Would I could say the maid that will.

"Hadst thou but been a daffodil
  That with the breezes sport and play,
For all thy suitor valued, still
  Thou so hadst danced thy life away.

"But thou so fair art chaste." Thus he
  Unto her answer answers e'er,
And that too in a way that she
  Must will or nill his answer hear.

And then a chair he'd ta'en, his chair
  Unto her side he nearer drew;
Recurr'd to memories sweet and rare,
  And in a softer key did woo.

"Must all the passion which I've sought
  So long to hide be paid with scorn?
A heart with pure affection fraught
  Be doomed a hopeless love to mourn?

"And must thou still its homage spurn?
　　And must thou still my suit reject?
And be to me this cruel thorn?
　　Reflect upon the past, reflect!

"A time there was, and time shall pass
　　To me ere that forgotten be,
When side by side from tide to tide
　　We played and sported on the lea.

"Ay, then have I not chased the bee
　　From bloom to bloom – oft chased and caught,
And having drawn its sting in glee,
　　To thee the little body brought?

"Then when a bloom of rarer dyes
　　Into my busy fingers fell,
To whom was reached the lucky prize?
　　Can not thy recollection tell?

"As oft away as summer went,
　　Who pulled with thee the haw, bright, brown –
Brown as thy own bright eyes – and bent
　　For thee the richest branches down?

"With blooms I've graced thy yellow hair,
　　With berries filled thy lap, thy hand, –
That hand as alabaster fair –
　　Had every gift at my command.

"Nay, tho' to others dour, yet meek
　　I ever was to thee, and kind;
And when we played at hide-and-seek, ·
　　I hid where thou would'st seek to find.

"Upon the playground still unmatched
　　Was I, unless my loved one played;
And then it seem'd to those who watched
　　My failures were on purpose made.

"As sure as e'er a race began,
　　The palm was mine unless she joined,
And then I always was out-ran,
　　For still with her I lagged behind.

"The ball I drove to others, mocked
　　Their efforts to arrest its flight;
But when my ball to her was knocked,
　　It would upon her lap alight.

"None, up and down so well I bobbed,
　　To skip the rope with me would try;
Did she attempt? my skill was robbed;
　　Another skipped her out – not I.

"At play thus was't; but childhood past,
　　And ere the lasses reach their teens,
Atween them and the lads a vast
　　Mysterious distance intervenes.

"They seldom on the green appear
　　In careless sport and play; and if
They join the throng erect they wear
　　Their head, and still their air is stiff

"They ail they know not what. And such
　　The change that on my lassie fell;
Then would she shrink my hand to touch,
　　And I half feared her touch as well.

"Had I changed too? This, I can tell, –
 That touch o'er me a spell would cast;
And did I pass her in the dell,
 With slow and snail-like pace I pass'd.

"Her voice had lost its former ring,
 Yet, in that voice such power was flung,
I better liked to hear her sing,
 Than when of old to me she sung.

"Her touch, her tone, would make or mar
 My bliss, and tho' with all my skill
I strove to please, and please but her,
 I in her presence blundered still.

"When by the hearth she sewing sat,
 Did I to thread her needle try?
Still, still my heart played pit-a-pat,
 And still I miss'd the needle's eye.

"As with the needle-threading, so
 We with the skein a-winding fared,
And Auntie's dreaded tongue would go
 Before the dancing end appeared.

"'What ails the lass?' she often said
 'She's sound asleep!' once said, and flew,
And snatched and snapt the tangled thread,
 While I – I know not how – withdrew.

"Away, too, fled those hours! Alack!
 They came and went like visions rare,
To mock the heart, delude and wrack,
 And leave the gazer in despair.

"Ah, less – tho' sun-illumed – less fair
    The blobs that dance adown the burn,
And let them burst they'll re-appear
    Ere those delightsome hours return.

"Yet they may live in thought, and could
    They live in Nettle's thought again,
Would she not change her bearing? would –
    Would she not change this bitter strain?

"Would she her lover still disdain?
    Would she continue thus to gall
And put him to this cruel pain?
    – Recall to mind the past, recall!"

Thus onward, on, his ditty flows,
    Until – her ruffled brow is sleek –
Till, lo! the lily drives the rose,
    The rose the lily from her cheek.

And now the iron, sparkling hot,
    Around with might and main he swings,
And down upon the proper spot
    With bang on bang the hammer brings!

"O, be my suit but undenied,
    And, ere the moon is on the wane,
A knot shall by the priest be tied,
    The priest shall never loose again.

"In heart and hand excell'd by none,
    Henceforth I'd front the ills of life;
And every victory I won
    Should be a jewel for my wife.

"So should the people of the dell,
    When they convened to gossip, say
For harmony we bore the bell,
    And bore it with a grace away.

"Nay, lift thy head, be not ashamed,
    If thus to feel – and thus, and O: –
As matters sinful might be blamed,
    Our saints were sinners long ago."

Deep silence here ensued. The cat,
    That lately to the nook had crept
To mark the sequel of their chat,
    Came forth – lay on the hearth and slept.

The needles bright, that left and right,
    As if with elfish glee possest,
Had gleamed and glanced, and frisked and danced,
    In quiet on her apron rest.

In concert with the storm within,
    The storm without forbears to blow;
And 'tween the sailing clouds, begin
    The joyous stars to come and go.

O'er all delight and silence brood,
    While to her wooer's bosom prest,
Poor Nettle's heart beats, beats aloud
    The tune that pleases lovers best.

And Thistle's pleased and Thistle's blest,
    And Thistle's is a joy supreme;
Ay! now of Nettle's smiles possest,
    He revels in a golden dream.

Dream on, brave youth; – An hour like this
    Annuls an age of cark and strife,
And turns into a drop of bliss
    The bitter cup of human life.

The tear is by a halo gilt,
    The thorns of life are turned to flowers,
The dirge into a merry lilt,
    When love returned for love is ours.

"I've heard," in language low and soft,
    Now Nettle's heart begins to flow; –
I've heard of honey'd tongues full oft,
    But never felt their force till now.

"Still would I fume, as day by day
    I've seen the lasses bought and sold
By some I'd scorn'd to own, had they
    Outweighed their very weight in gold.

"My hour of triumph's o'er. In vain
    Did I my fellow-maids abuse;
I've snatched the cup, and drank the bane
    Which sets me in their very shoes;

"That turns a heart of adamant
    To pliant wax; and, in my turn,
Subjects me to the bitter taunt,
    The vanquished victor's ever borne;

"That leaveth Nettle satisfied
    To leave her kith and kin, and by
Her ever-faithful Thistle's side,
    To shelter till the day they die."

It sounded in castle and palace,
    It sounded in cottage and shed,
It sped over mountains and valleys,
    And withered the earth as it sped;
Like a blast in its fell consummation
    Of all that we holy should hold,
Thrilled, thrilled thro' the nerves of the nation,
    A cry for the reign of King Gold.

Upstarted the chiefs of the city,
    And sending it back with a ring,
To the air of a popular ditty,
    Erected a throne to the king;
'Twas based upon fiendish persuasions,
    Cemented by crimes manifold:
Embellished by specious ovations,
    That dazzled the foes of King Gold.

The prey of unruly emotion,
    The miner and diver go forth,
And the depths of the earth and the ocean
    Are shorn of their lustre and worth;
The mountain is riven asunder,
    The days of the valley are told;
And sinew, and glory, and grandeur,
    Are sapped for a smile of King Gold.

Beguiled of their native demeanour,
    The high rush with heirlooms and bays,
The poor with what gold cannot weigh, nor
    The skill of the pedant appraise;

The soldier he spurs with his duty,
  And lo! by the frenzy made bold,
The damsel she glides with her beauty,
  To garnish the brow of King Gold.

Accustomed to traffic forbidden
  By honour – by heaven – each hour,
The purest, by conscience unchidden,
  Laugh, laugh at the noble and pure;
And Chastity, rein'd in a halter,
  Is led to the temple and sold, –
Devotion herself, at the altar,
  Yields homage alone to King Gold.

Affection on whose honey blossom,
  The child of affliction still fed –
Affection is plucked from the bosom,
  And malice implanted instead;
And dark grow the brows of the tender,
  And colder the hearts of the cold: –
Love, pity, and justice surrender
  Their charge of the hounds of King Gold.

See, see, from the sear'd earth ascending,
  A cloud o'er the welkin expands;
See, see, 'mid the dense vapour bending,
  Pale women with uplifted hands;
Smokes thus to the bridegroom of Circe,
  The dear blood of hundreds untold;
Invoke thus the angel of mercy,
  A curse on the reign of King Gold.

It sounded in castle and palace,
  It sounded in cottage and shed,

It sped over mountains and valleys,
    And withered the earth as it sped;
Like a blast in its fell consummation,
    Of all that we holy should hold,
Thrilled, thrilled thro' the nerves of the Nation;
    "Cling! Clang! for the reign of King Gold."

EPISTLE TO JOSEPH SKIPSEY
By William Reay
(*See Biographical Notes pp. 52-56 above*)

'Tis three and twenty summers past
Since you and I apart were cast
To fight the cold world's bitter blast,
    As some folk call it;
But let's be cheerful till the last,
    Whate'er befall it.

I know this world has many a jar,
As rugged as the flinty scaur
Which drives the poet's raptures far
    Beyond his guiding;
And yet the heart that knows no war
    Has little biding.

It needs but little wit to know it:
This is no land for musing poet:
The cricket ball, the people show it
    To be their glory;
Or how some boatsman's skill, "be blow it,"
    Fills all their story.

Yet what's the good of whining, wailing,
Or gathering evils for retailing!
Our vessel's whole! let her keep sailing!
    All weathers past!
We'll find some worthy pilot hailing
    Us safe at last.

Here we are still; then let us know
There's pleasure in all winds that blow
O'er summer hills, or winter snow,
    By night, by day;
And glory in the western glow
    Stealing away.

And in the silent hours of night,
When moon and stars are shining bright,
With whom our souls in raptured flight,
    Loves oft to roam:
Seeking amid their sacred light
    A lasting home.

And golden morn with glittering train,
When Phoebus wakes to light again —
The nibbling flocks, the whistling swain,
    The woodman strong,
And reapers, mong the golden grain
    Chanting their song.

A heart-felt song, high up ascending,
A charm unto the landscape lending,
And birds in joyous mirth contending
    Among the trees;
While Autumn tints harmonious blending
    Wave in the breeze.

Through such fair visions would I stray,
Till wandering by the Wier's green way,
Where thy fine harp was wont to play,
    Beneath those walls,
Whose towering heights like giants grey,
    Old time recalls.

To hear thy tales of ancient times,
Of holy men, and kingly crimes,
The while the grand Cathedral* chimes,   **Durham Cathedral,*
    Would pour their song,   *County Durham.*
Like poet's flights in loftiest rhymes,
    Floating along.

There many a theme did once engage
Thy thoughts upon that antique page,
Where holy men, and bearded sage
    Their legends pour,
A city full of hoary age—
    Grim ancient lore.

But yet amid that busy throng
Of ancient saints in shadows long,
Or heroes moved by passions strong
    In bye gone times:
The sweetest theme should be thy song
    In graphic rhymes.

Such quiet joys I'd seek with thee,
That's found by lonely lake and lea,
Where spells that fall from tower and tree
    And flowerets fine,
Might swell thy songs so dear to me
    To many a line.

Two pilgrims still; we'd cross the Tyne,
Past wooded glens and castles fine,
To see the Wandsbeck waters shine—
    Sweet be their flow!
As dear to this fond heart of mine,
    Long years ago.

168

Dear cousin Bob and Ephraim too,
Whose simple hearts were kind and true,
Oft wandered with us through and through
    Those pleasant rambles:
When tired, we drank till we were fu',
    At Collin Campb'll's.*   *An Hotel at Choppington,
                                           near Bedlington.

I like a joyous hour to spend
With social glass and genial friend,
For then our darkest cares will wend
    We know not whither,
To see our happiest feelings blend
    With one another.

Were we among our native hills,
Where bonnie Couquett stream distills,
And Wandsbeck, queen of sparkling rills,
    And hawthorns scented —
We'd whet again our blunted quills,
    And live contented.

We'd muse upon each place and time,
Where all things bear the glow of rhyme,
Where every bush and tree can chime
    The raptured story,
Which fire the youth in every clime
    To love and glory.

Whose mountain, summit, glen, and cave,
Speak of the glories of the brave,
Who marched forth like the stemless wave,
    'Mid battle's clang;
Laying down the tyrants, and the slave,
    In layers alang.

O! then, sweet muse, harmonious maid,
Could I for once but win thine aid,
To touch those glorious scenes portrayed
    In ancient story,
Where sternest warriors deep did wade
    Through blood to glory!

Fair gentle Muse, take thou my hand,
Lead me to that bright fairy land
Where near to Nature I may stand
    In musing mood,
And every natural charm command,
    By field and flood.

Or to some calm immortal shrine,
Where those who loved and sang recline,
The glory of the radiant Nine,
    In sweet repose;
Where every art in grace combine,
    And genius glows.

Yes! were I young, I might aspire,
To touch that mighty swelling lyre,
That wins all hearts; the heart-felt fire,
    Which all men know,
Should be my theme, should me inspire,
    In joy or woe.

But ah! I fear that time's gone by,
That lit the flame in you and I,
Which gave a light to every sky
    And streamlet glancing,
And sent the spirits dancing high,
    Like coursers prancing.

Now like a barque with folded sail,
I drift before life's rustling gale;
Still would I chant some cheerful tale,
    As long's I may
And with my genial friend still hail
    Each closing day.

To sit with thee beside the fire,
When day with all its toils retire,
To hear thee sweep the passionate lyre,
    The heart revealing,
Warming the soul till it inspire
    The holiest feeling.

What then were courts, kingdoms, and state,
The gilded name that sounds so great,
The boiling wine, the costly plate,
    The dazzling glare,
Have oft been found, alas! too late —
    Not worth their care.

Keep to thy muse, my gentle crony,
Still weave those lines so soft and bonnie,
Of lovers' woes, and gossips funny,
    Until we meet,
When o'er each tale, dearer than money,
    We'll laugh and greet.

W. REAY.

To W. R.
A Friend in Australia.

O wily Willie Reay, I've read
Your book of rhymes, and be it said
Few sweeter rhymes were ever made
    To grace our tongue
Since Burns, with Scotia's Muse's aid,
    His ditties sung.

The bonnie banks of Wanie's burn,
With Bothal's Castle, old and stern,
And fane revered where in an urn
    Of fame's yet shown,
Engage your charming muse in turn
    With scenes less known.

The coy bell-blooms in purple dark, –
Shade-loving mays that seem to hark
To what the skyward soaring lark
    May o'er them sing, –
You in the wood with pleasure mark
    Return each Spring.

Delighted, too, you see unclose
The petals of the pale primrose;
The sweetest flower that comes and goes,
    While – life to bear!
Yet down the glen the blackbird blows
    His whistle clear.

E'en so your heart dirls to behold
The little daisy's charms unfold,
As when with me in days of old,

172

Its blooms among,
You heard the linnet's love-tale told
    In many a song.

O'er these and scenes like these you brood;
And when wrapt in a higher mood,
The aidance of the muse is sued,
    Then, then behold;
Their living pictures many-hued
    Your lines unfold.

Nor less to you than Wanie rare,
The banks of Wear, beyond compare,
For castles grand, whose towers yet wear
    The airs they wore,
When steel-girt enemies drew near,
    In days of yore.

There Lumley bold to Lambton shows
A front that almost threatens blows;
And Lambton up the valley throws
    A look at him,
With which her lords once answered foes
    In battle grim.

But scenes of war and war's alarms,
Proud prancing steeds and knights at arms,
And other founts of human harms,
    Ah, let us fly
To scenes of peace; – still, these have charms
    Far you and I.

Away, away then let us steer
Our courses higher up the Wear,
To where old Finchale's ruins dear,
    For ages vast,
Have looked into the waters clear,
    That gurgle past.

Beneath yon trees once grim and stern –
Which seem in fancy's ken to yearn
For days that were when they would spurn
    And backward beat
The fiercest blast that blew – we'll turn
    And take a seat.

Upon the crispy fern we'll rest
And gaze upon the scene possest
Of what is sweetest, dearest, best,
    To souls like ours;
The winding slopes in verdure drest –
    The trees and flowers.

Hard by in shade the foxglove dwells,
And rears on high her purple bells,
From which, when wind-a-dangled, wells
    In fancy's ear
An air no mortal air excels,
    Nor yet can peer.

There may one see the poppy burn
Amid the yet green waving corn;
And when the yellow grain is shorn,
    We yet may see
This black-eyed crimson queen adorn
    In tufts the lea.

Blue-bottles too, whose tender hue
Will match the sky's own lovely blue,
Upon an early morn, we'll view,
    A pleasure rare:
But how can I describe to you
    What we'll see there?

There, there upon a holiday,
Will toilers in their best array,
Come with their little ones to play,
    A pleasant sight;
And many a prank is played ere day
    Hath taken flight.

There, on some bonnie afternoon,
While bees awake a drowsy tune;
Or, later on, while cushats croon
    A heartfelt lay,
And o'er them hangs the yellow moon,
    Will lovers stray.

In such an hour it were a treat
To hear our minstrel's self repeat
His May Morning, in accents meet;
    That carol true,
And one more musical and sweet,
    I never knew.

The gift to warble such a song
Can but to Nature's bards belong,
With whom we'd rather dree the prong
    Of Want's grim self,
Than revel with yon gilded throng
    That worship pelf.

Ah! never crony let us fash
Our heads about a lot of cash;
Nor seek with sparks to cut a dash;
    Compared, I say,
What are the gauds they prize but trash
    To one sweet lay.

This, when away yon castles proud
Have vanished like some ragged cloud,
That nor'-land winds a-piping loud
    Have o'er them blown,
May yet to hearts by labour bowed
    A joy be known.

And such a lay let me aver
Will prove "May Morning" or I err;
And "Jenny," too, tho' I prefer
    To this a third;
E'en that wherein you curse the cur
    That shot the bird.

All these are very sweet and fine,
And to my palate, precious wine,
And every stanza, every line,
    As water clear,
Awakes a melody divine
    To charm the ear.

But end I must; awhile adieu
To you and those so dear to you;
And hinney, Willie, kiss them, do,
    Your bairns and wife,
In kind remembrance of your true,
    Fond friend for life.

To W. R. II
A Friend in Australia.

To you, on you, my Willy Reay,
To you, on you, so many a day,
Out o'er the seas and far away, –
    A word or two,
A wee to ease my heart, I'd say
    A word on you.

In this my wifie's thought's express'd,
For well I know within her breast
She ranks you with the truest, best
    Of friends that I
Possess, or ever yet possest
    In days gone by.

We've had our troubles great and small
Since last we met you, but 'mid all
We've thought of you and yours, and shall,
    While life endures,
With rapture sweet the names recall
    Of you and yours.

And often in the night-tide hours,
When, toil-relieved, and memory pours
Into our souls her sweetest showers,
    Her healing dew,
Distilled from joy and sorrow's flowers,
    We'll talk of you.

Of all the funny tales you'd tell
About the folks upon the Fell,

Where Teams flows onward yet to swell
    Our own dear Tyne,
We'll talk as if beneath a spell
    Almost divine.

The twinkle of your eye when aught
Grotesque or sweet your fancy caught,
And ended in some happy thought,
    Or feeling deep;
Of this with painful pleasure fraught,
    We'll talk and weep.

Your jokes that never left a sting,
Of your bright laugh, whose merry ring
Told of the pureness of its spring,
    The hours away,
We'll talk, talk, talk of every thing
    You'd do or say.

Nor only of the joys that were,
But what the golden hour will bear
When you return, we'll talk; for ne'er,
    Befall what may,
Can we of your return despair,
    Nay, never! nay.

That cruel thought we could not dree,
That cruel thought we'll flee and flee,
Till you again have cross'd the sea;
    For come you will,
And with your heart-inspiring glee,
    Our feelings thrill.

Then will we mock at curst mischance,
And sing our song and dance our dance;
And on our native hobbies prance,
 Unlike yon crew
Who merely ape the apes of France
 In all they do.

A little fun will oft engage
The moments of the deepest sage;
And tho' we're somewhat touched with age,
 Our jokes we'll crack, –
Nay, Glee on Care a war will wage
 When you come back.

As wont, we'll ramble up and down
Our smoky and yet rare old town;
Most rare I say, and with a frown
 What! Willy, what!
Would we not face a king or clown,
 Would say it's not?

We'll down and see the castle grand,
So firmly built, so nobly planned;
And at whose feet two bridges stand,
 Of rare design,
By which from bank to bank is spann'd,
 Our Coaly Tyne.

We'll see St. Nicholas as of old,
For beauty worth its weight in gold,
Nor heed if others suns behold,
 In fanes afar,
To which compared our own, we're told
 Is but a star.

Confound the carpers who compare
The virtues of our jewels fair,
As if they loved away to scare
     Some vision which
Might otherwise with magic rare
     Our lives enrich!

Have we not ills enough and more,
But we must keep a bolted door,
Lest some stray fay from Beauty's shore,
     Of Love begot,
Glide in to charm us evermore?
     La! have we not?

But whither flies the Muse? A throng
Of feelings hurries her along;
Yet like the tinkler in the song,
     In all her flight,
Just when she seems to go most wrong,
     She goes most right!

Your nags so hide-bound, stiff, and tough,
May suit old hags, gaunt, grim, and gruff,
But not the gipsy elves, enough,
     Whose spirits high
Would into airy nothing puff
     The world they fly!

On winged steeds they'd go; nor will
Our Muse less swift scour onward still,
When thrill our heart-strings as they thrill,
     Nay, almost crack,
At thought of how the time we'll kill
     When you come back!

We'll then, as I have said and say,
The glories of our town survey;
A visit to the Dene we'll pay;
    Then down the burn
We'll link ho! ho! we'll link that day,
    When you return.

Away to canny Shields will we,
And bonny Whitley-by-the-Sea,
Then up to Hexham in our glee;
    Nay, rest we'll spurn
Till all the country-side we see,
    When you return.

That will we view, and many a thing
To which our sweetest feelings cling,
And from our harps shall flow a spring
    From rapture born,
That many a lad and lass shall sing,
    When you return.

When you return; when Mary Jane
And you come sailing o'er the main,
No storm will blow the ship to strain –
    Each charm-bound wave
Will duck its head down till you gain
    Our harbour safe.

That day of days? – Run, Sally, run!
And stop the tune in love begun,
Or I shall harp till I'm undone,
    And have, alack!
No strength to hug our cronies, none!
    When they come back.

Not, not so fast. Ah, there, now there,
You've bumped your chin against the chair
And bit your tongue – well I declare!
    That tongue that's rung
Me many a curtain song so rare,
    Since we were young.

"Ha, ha!" you cry: well, darling, well,
I'm glad that naught occurr'd to quell
The music of that golden bell,
    And that its clack
May help my welcome cry to swell
    When Will comes back.

Till then, again, adieu, my friend,
And when you have an hour to spend
On rhyme, a rhyme thy crony send:
    Do, Willy do;
Meanwhile, believe me to the end,
    A brother true.

Bill McCumiskey B.Sc
(Psychology), B.Sc [sic]
(Spanish), M.A. is a time-served
sheet metal worker and welder,
born in the East End of
Newcastle upon Tyne in 1950.
His book of short stories, *The
Peanuts of Agincourt*, was
published in 2009.

Kelsey Thornton has been
Professor of English and Head of
Department at the Universities of
Newcastle upon Tyne and
Birmingham, and now lives in
Newcastle editing, drawing, and
writing poems

Chris Harrison is a music
education consultant, workshop
leader and performer. In 2010 he
started setting some of his great-
great-grandfather's poems to
music, and has been giving
performances of these songs as a
way of raising awareness of
Joseph Skipsey's achievements.